YOU CAN'T MAKE "FISH CLIMB TREES"

Overcoming Educational Malpractice through Authentic Learning

You will and have always been a great inspiration. So thank you for the support. Hope you find this book a great read.

LAWRENCE MUGANGA Ph.D.
FOREWORD BY STEVE REVINGTON

Suite 300 - 990 Fort St
Victoria, BC, V8V 3K2
Canada

www.friesenpress.com

Copyright © 2018 by Lawrence Muganga
First Edition — 2018

All rights reserved.

No part of this publication may be reproduced in any form, or by any means, electronic or mechanical, including photocopying, recording, or any information browsing, storage, or retrieval system, without permission in writing from FriesenPress.

www.lawrencemuganga.com

ISBN
978-1-5255-2534-6 (Hardcover)
978-1-5255-2535-3 (Paperback)
978-1-5255-2536-0 (eBook)

1. Education, Teaching Methods & Materials

Distributed to the trade by The Ingram Book Company

ENDORSEMENTS

"With global contemporary educational systems almost entirely modeled on the modernist and rationalist learning structures where learning is formulated and implemented as an open competition among students, irrespective of the specific backgrounds and prevailing need of the participants, Lawrence Muganga produces an important, timely book that rightly advises us to rethink this. With his culturally and contextually responsive observations and analyses, we shall do well to heed his call for new epistemologies and methodologies of education that can offer us the promise as well as the pragmatics of creative learning, which especially in relation to postcolonial Sub-Saharan Africa, are urgently needed. This is a must-read book for educators and everyone who cares about creating an education experience that is relevant to real-life and sticks with students for a lifetime."

Ali A. Abdi, PhD
Professor of Social Development Education & Department Head,
Department of Educational Studies
Faculty of Education
University of British Columbia

"This is a fantastic book that is refreshing and touches on almost every major aspects and challenges to education in the 21st Century. The book does a great job juxtaposing educational experiences in the west (Canada) and Sub-Saharan Africa. I am hoping and praying hard that it will turn out to be a best seller."

Andrew Ojede, PhD
Professor of Economics
Department of Finance & Economics McCoy College of Business Administration
Texas State University
Texas, USA

> The book *'You Can't Make Fish Climb Trees'* skilfully encapsulates the essence of authentic learning and why educational institutions should aim to achieve authentic learning. Using authentic examples based on his own experiences, Lawrence Muganga explains not only what authentic learning is, and why it is important for educators to facilitate authentic learning, but also provides practical information on how to implement authentic learning. A must read for postsecondary educators.

Heather Kanuka, PhD
Professor, Educational Policy Studies
University of Alberta
Canada

> "With his book, *You Can't Make "Fish Climb Trees"*, Lawrence Muganga masterfully explains the universal need and working components of authentic learning. He also genuinely understands that an authentic learning approach is the way of education's future. His description of authentic learning as a living, breathing model of education sums up his great appreciation for this potent style of learning. Importantly, it also reveals his deep respect for genuine learning in this vast and interconnected world."

Steve Revington,
The Pioneer and leader of Authentic Learning, is an Educator and Author, Winner of the Canadian Prime Minister's Award of Teaching Excellence (2016) and was selected as a top fifty finalist for the inaugural Global Teacher Prize (2015). Steve's work can be found at: authenticlearningweebly.com. Twitter: @AuthenticEduc
Ontario, Canada

"In a world where many school graduates are "graduates on paper but with no salient hands on or soft skills training", The book *You Can't Make "Fish Climb Trees"* is a true reflection of the hard and piercing reality of our school system and most graduates that emerge from it. Both the teacher and student may be very well schooled but not skilled in their locus. The education given to them in most cases does not suit the terrain they find themselves in and as a Bantu proverb goes "you can't not bend an already grown tree .or make a fish crawl on land" The book gives us formidable ground to reflect on the role of a teacher and student as pivots for authentic and inauthentic learning in Sub Saharan Africa. These are the people who will climb the tree if allowed to climb trees at the very inception of their education. This book provides needed fundamental ground for meaningful engagement on curriculum and pedagogical reform to support real-life learning that solves real world problems."

Muwagga Mugagga Anthony, PhD
Professor of Philosophy of Education
Ag. Director Institute of Education Research (IER)
Makerere University College of Education and External Studies

"*You Can't Make "Fish Climb Trees"* represents an articulation of a long over-due new direction in educational policy and practice for the 21st century socio-economic order. It is a ground-breaking conversation starter that advocates a breakaway from "moribund" educational system to a new revolutionary frontier compatible with today's world economic realities. It is thought-provoking and makes an easy read. Highly recommended!"

Bede Eke, PhD
Professor of Sociology,
Department of Sociology,
University of Alberta

DEDICATION

This book is dedicated to the following people:

To my mother, Immaculate: There are no satisfying words in this world that can express how I feel about you – because of you, I am and I'm always thankful to the Heavenly Father for he chose you to be my mom. You toiled for us, endured unbearable poverty and suffering just for us and in process you taught me one important trait – to do the best I can with my life and be of use to society. This book is the product of all your sacrifices and it's my prayer that it is of use to society.

To my miracle wife, Eve: Who has always accepted me for me and supported my hustles, ambition, and drive. What a dependable partner to have in this journey called life – you are and always will be my impeccable wife and mother to our children. Without your support, it's possible this book may not have seen the light of day.

To you revered readers, this book has come to life because of you and is for you – without you it's unrealistic to even imagine the existence of this book! Thank you for choosing to join the conversation about re-defining our perspectives on education and advocating for an Authentic Learning Education Model compatible with today's world socio-economic realities, which seeks to prepare students for the real world by equipping them with real-life skills they need to face challenges of now and the unpredictable future.

TABLE OF CONTENTS

Foreword by Steve Revington	xi
Prologue	xv
CHAPTER ONE: TALES OF EDUCATIONAL MALPRACTICE	1
CHAPTER TWO: HISTORY OF EDUCATIONAL PHILOSOPHY	29
CHAPTER THREE: AUTHENTIC LEARNING	47
CHAPTER FOUR: EDUCATION IN AFRICA	69
CHAPTER FIVE: AUTHENTIC LEARNING IN SSA	87
CHAPTER SIX: THE CREATIVE ECONOMY	101
CHAPTER SEVEN: BENEFITS OF AUTHENTIC LEARNING	117
CHAPTER EIGHT: IMPLEMENTING AUTHENTIC LEARNING IN SSA	133
Conclusion	153
References	157
Acknowledgements	175

FOREWORD
BY STEVE REVINGTON

Authentic learning is not a new concept, as learning by doing has been a hallmark of apprenticeships and genuine skill development since ancient times. It has however, been greatly lost and misunderstood and had all but disappeared since the dawning of the industrial era.

This industrialized learning model became a reflection of the mass production lines that developed during the end of the nineteenth century, characterized by a "one-size-fits-all" approach in education. This approach may have served a purpose, to meet the demands of an industrial based era, but societal and economical expectations have evolved immensely, and we now find ourselves searching for new paradigms in education that will prepare our students effectively for the future.

I loved the pursuit of education but didn't really like school. I was, however, lucky to have a few teachers on my education journey that provided me with creative sparks, meaningful connections that fired my curiosity, and provided me with glimpses into the exciting possibilities of what education could be.

Small glimpses, such as my grade seven teacher, Mr. Ken Myles, who provided our history class with learning stations to recreate major events of The War of 1812. My group chose to create a short-recorded vignette on a cassette about the British advance towards Washington, complete with script, self-generated sound effects, multiple speaking roles and narration. I remember how each student was so excited and motivated to complete our task and how time flew during those classes. We not only read the assigned passages in our texts, but we gravitated to other resources in the room to confirm what we had written in our script. Here we were writing, rehearsing our lines and delving into history in an adventurous way and doing so via a medium we had only dreamed about.

What a far better learning experience from the usual writing down of endless notes off the numerous chalkboards, then being tested at the end of the unit about the names, dates and events we pretended to understand. Our imaginations were kindled, and our passions were spurred on by purposeful, relevant expectations and a time sensitive deadline. As I'm writing this, I'm still surprised at the details I can recall about this one-time assignment that took place almost fifty years ago.

Multi-sensory, integrated, interactive, collaborative and relevant learning, is learning that sticks. Best of all, it's a style of learning that lays a solid foundation for additional topic expertise. It develops skill sets that are transferable to other experiences, motivates and builds confidence in learners and is personalized learning. Early in my teaching career I tried to introduce my students to learning initiatives that provided that same excitement I'd experienced on my War of 1812 assignment. After several years of implementing authentic events such as Living Museums, The Egg Drop Project, Passion Projects, Themed Dinner Theaters, Robotic Challenges, to name a few, I started to observe clear and consistent characteristics. I called these the Elements of Authentic Learning. Over and over, regardless of the subject area, gender, age, economic, cultural or academic levels I discovered that the closer a student's learning was to "real-life" scenarios the more passionate, engaged, motivated, team-based and academically inclined they became.

When students are immersed in audience driven initiatives, producing purposeful, tangible outcomes, collaborating and consulting with people with relevant and expert skill sets, while pursuing personalized experiences, then learning becomes optimal. When academics are strategically aligned with these initiatives, then a student's educational experience can be significantly amplified.

It's important to note that when we are talking about creating these initiatives we're talking about creating real-world events with all their warts and their wonders. That's the beauty of authentic education, it really is real. I identified twelve reoccurring elements that were consistently present in each authentic event implemented, and there may be even more depending on the initiative. As we team up with our students, staffs, parents, community and expert contributors we are set upon a journey full of triumphs and challenges as it significantly hones student preparedness for life itself. Isn't that the purpose of education in the first place, to prepare students for life?

Until an educator has taken on this journey, it's difficult to comprehend the significant effects that authentic learning practices can have on students. It is as rewarding as it is demanding but the rewards are significant and lasting. Sitting in a chair, regurgitating information in a control environment is static learning. It's purpose is realized upon the completion of a test and its impact is fleeting. Authentic learning is about addressing students holistically, as it is only when we address the 'real' that we're able to address the whole.

With his book, You Can't Make "Fish Climb Trees", Lawrence Muganga masterfully explains the universal need and working components of authentic learning. He also genuinely understands that an authentic learning approach is the way of education's future.

His description of authentic learning as a living, breathing model of education sums up his great appreciation for this potent style of learning. Importantly, it also reveals his deep respect for genuine learning in this vast and interconnected world. Learning can no longer be the divisive agent it has grown to be. With it's fragmented subjects, strict time schedules, superficial, short-term memory exercises, mainly devoid of deep, ongoing connectivity with the outside world, this industrial age framed education era is nearing its end. Lawrence Muganga embraces this positive awakening and would like to do his part in correcting the errors of the past and forging a positive future of possibilities.

It wasn't long, after my first talk with Lawrence, that I recognized his acute understanding and deep, rooted passion for authentic learning and his desire to actively promote AL to education systems. His belief that authentic learning teaches both minds and the hearts of students is a shared belief with other great educators I've been fortunate to work with over the years.

His belief in an education that honours a student's uniqueness, through personalized learning is a driving force to promote authentic learning experiences. In this way he believes that students can make genuine connections, immerse themselves in valued, engaging initiatives and attain skill sets that are aligned with useful, temporal needs.

In an ever-changing world our students need to be flexible, critical thinking problem solvers with real experiences to draw upon to be able to adapt and thrive. Lawrence's book provides an excellent template for educators wanting to understand education's past and a map to positively navigate towards an authentic learning model. His wish for education's future - is to nurture and support the realization of every student's greatest aspirations through the opportunities that only authentic learning experiences can provide.

Steve Revington is a pioneer and leader of Authentic Learning. He has designed, implemented and promoted a wide variety of authentic education initiatives, most notably The Egg Drop Project. He's written articles, produced videos, and currently hosts Google's number one website on Authentic Learning. He received a TV Ontario Teacher's Award for his innovative practices (1994), an Associate Teachers Award of Excellence from The University of Western Ontario (2013) and was selected as a top fifty finalist for the inaugural Global Teacher Prize (2015). He received Canada's Prime Minister's Award of Teaching Excellence (2016) and promotes Authentic Learning as an educational speaker, author and consultant.

PROLOGUE

From educator Steve Revington to creativity apologist Sir Ken Robinson, many scholars and educators have pointed out the failings of the modern school system. Beginning in nineteenth century Europe, governments and administrators structured and delivered education to mirror a type of assembly line, where children were pushed through rooms and delivered mass-produced education that completely discounted individual differences. This paradigm shift resulted from structural functionalist sociological thought that "perceived the human psyche as shaped quite fundamentally by social institutions" (Dobbin, 2009, p. 206). The idea that social institutions such as workplaces and schools could standardize and homogenize the population towards a goal of industrial efficiency has created a system of education that award-winning Canadian educator Steve Revington (2016) refers to as "a traditional industrial age modality" (para. 3) and Ken Robinson (2010) dubs "mass produced education." Interestingly, both scholars envision the education system developed 150 years ago as a factory, thus reflecting the institutional perspective from the nineteenth century.

Today, much of the world has evolved beyond this institutional mode of thinking, with the economy shifting from a manufacturing to a service-based or knowledge-based economy and technology advancing from rotary wall phones to the iPhone X or horse-and-carriage transportation to sleek SUVs. However, schools, from kindergarten to postgraduate education, have remained relatively unchanged.

We have all been there, inside the neatly ordered classrooms, struggling to sit still behind a desk, and listening to the teacher drone on and on and on about meaningless facts. Gnawing at the end of our pencils, rocking back in our chairs, passing notes to our friends, and wondering when it will end, not just the day, but that final bell that propels us into the world of work.

For many of us, it lasts anywhere from twelve to twenty years before we need to get out there and find what society terms a "real job." But what is a real job? For decades or even centuries, that "real job" was merely an extension of school: more order, more rules, more structure. More following orders, but from the boss rather than the teacher. More sitting at a desk.

Fortunately, the world has changed; the workforce has undergone a gradual shift from a manufacturing economy to one that emphasizes knowledge and creativity. This type of economy, coined the "creative economy" by John Howkins (2001), involves the creation and dissemination of products and services that involve or overlap with creative industries as well as the injection of creativity and innovation into many traditional fields. Within this new marketplace, increasing numbers of people are starting their own businesses and finding their own niches in the workforce. But while the labor force now allows people to chase their dreams, the education system, which remains mired in the past, a relic of an earlier world, provides a barrier to these dreams.

Around the world, students still sit at desks and listen to the teacher "vicariously discussing topics and regurgitating information" that will never help them land that dream job or start their own business (Revington, 2016). Like I did thirty years ago, students still burn the midnight oil memorizing names, dates, and places, and then spit that information back out on year-end examinations that purport to determine their worth in the world. Then, they attempt the daunting task of finding a job or continuing their fruitless quest for more education. More desks, more teachers, more tests. The cycle never ends.

Astonishingly, the education system remains static despite overwhelming evidence that demonstrates the desperate need for change. Educational philosophies showing the inadequacy of teacher-centered learning date more than a hundred years back, even when the "industrial modality" still constituted a relatively vogue style of education. John Dewey, one of the pioneers of constructivism as an educational theory, proposed the idea of student-centered learning nearly a century ago. Dewey, along with his successors, suggested a teaching approach that envisioned students at the center of the learning, where teachers provided them with control over their own education and tailored the learning to their strengths, interests, and needs. In fact, Dewey proposed that children "construct" their knowledge by building or "scaffolding" their learning based on prior knowledge in incremental stages (Lewis & Williams, 1994; McLeod, 2015; Peterson, 2002). This paradigm, which subsequently became known as student-centered learning, eventually diverged into distinct learning methodologies.

One of these approaches, which evolved into authentic learning, maintains that teachers must provide a realistic context for learning by taking learning outside the bounds of the classroom and connecting it with the "real world." Authentic learning arguably first originated from Canadian educator Steve Revington and Australian academic Jan Herrington, both of whom proposed a series of principles and characteristics that defined this mode of education (Revington, 2016; Herrington, 2009). These traits will undergo further discussion within Chapter 3, which focuses exclusively on situating and characterizing authentic learning.

Although student-centered learning and its affiliate theories have existed for nearly a century, educators, even in developed parts of the world, have failed to fully implement student-centered learning within the education systems of these countries. Isolated and fragmented initiatives that connect the classroom with the real world have begun to occur at various levels, within provinces and states, and in various classrooms, programs, and schools, some of which merit mentioning in the subsequent chapters. Nevertheless, wholesale efforts that attempt to revolutionize the education system from an industrial, teacher-centered system of learning to a delivery mode characterized largely by student-centered learning remain ineffectual despite literature that attests to the enormous benefits of authentic learning, discussed in Chapter 7.

While developed countries have increased the number of student-centered initiatives in the form of instructional delivery and practical activities due to their relatively plentiful resources, third-world countries lack the money, knowledge, and technology to properly implement student-centered, and, more specifically, authentic learning. In Sub-Saharan Africa (SSA), one of the poorest regions in the world, authentic learning remains a largely unknown concept. The lack of resources in these countries present one of the greatest barriers to implementing authentic learning, as Chapters 4 and 5 will detail.

As an individual who was born, raised, and educated in Uganda, I have personally experienced the education system in these countries from Primary 1 (Grade 1) to my Master's Degree. In fact, my vignette in the first chapter takes the reader through the journey that I underwent in navigating the school system and struggling to translate that education into the real world. My Canadian colleague, Aviah, who shared her story with me, took a startlingly similar path within the supposedly advanced Canadian school system. As you will read, both of us have experienced the teacher-centered, homogenized education that fails to connect to the real world and leaves students stranded in the job market. Although my colleague's story seems to diverge from the focus on SSA education, it shows that the same type of educational malpractice underlying SSA schooling, which originated in nineteenth century Europe, has permeated throughout the world. The spread of educational malpractice, along with the resources deficit in underdeveloped countries, accounts for the fact that while developed nations have made some minor shifts towards student-centered learning, SSA still remains mired in an ancient system with ancient technology and a complete paucity of human, financial, or knowledge capital to make any changes.

Although the school system has failed us and countless other students around the world, it is never too late for change. The emerging knowledge-based or creative economy, discussed extensively in Chapter 6, requires that individuals manipulate knowledge through the mastery of skills such as critical thinking, problem solving, decision-making, analysis, collaboration, communication, innovation, and creativity (Sawyer, 2008). However, schools have largely failed to adapt to this crucial change, and still remain designed for a manufacturing economy. In order to bring schools into the modern era and prepare students for the creative economy, the education systems throughout the world require wholesale changes in terms of curriculum, instructional strategies, and delivery methods. In particular, SSA, which suffers from numerous skills gaps in several industries, including healthcare, education, and agriculture (Binagwaho et al., 2013; Materu, 2007; United Nations, 2011), needs to adopt authentic learning. By adopting authentic learning, African schools can provide students with the necessary soft skills that are needed to succeed in the corporate or entrepreneurial world.

Accordingly, this book advocates for the importance of integrating authentic learning into the school systems in SSA as a way of preparing students for the creative economy and the soft skills required within this economic paradigm (Sawyer, 2008). The stakeholders of this book are many, and as such, the intended audience includes not only government members, administrators, and educational researchers but also teachers, instructors, students, parents, employers, entrepreneurs, and anyone who cares about education. Despite its focus on SSA, people in western countries can still strongly benefit from understanding authentic learning, the creative economy, and how the former can help to bridge the increasing chasm between school and society. In addition, by targeting the book towards a secondary western audience, I hope to convince North American and European readers to assist SSA regions by whatever means necessary, including knowledge-sharing, open-source materials, technology, and financial resources.

The material that guides this book's arguments originates not merely from scholarly and academic literature but also from the personal experiences of many individuals, including myself and the people with whom I have had contact, as well as from the world of popular culture. My ongoing doctoral study has served as a major source of inspiration for this book, and, as such, I have included interviews from Ugandan university instructors as evidence for the current state of the school system in SSA. In addition to incorporating different types of sources from personal to impersonal, from scholarly to popular, some of the sources come from western and nonwestern countries, underscoring the fact that while Africa remains the focal region of this study, the same problem concerning the mismatch between education and economy plagues most of the world. Despite the broad diversity of sources incorporated in this book, the message remains the same.

The objectives of the book are twofold: 1) to teach readers about the inadequacies of the school system and its inability to transition graduates to the workforce mostly in SSA but also throughout the world and 2) to stimulate conversation in the form of future research, policy proposals, and other preliminary steps that will initiate change. The long-term objective of this book ideally envisions a wholesale change in the way that education is conceived and delivered, allowing students around the world to realize their dreams both in school and in life.

Before discussing the research that informed this book, I will recount the stories that prompted the need for change. So, let us begin our journey.

CHAPTER ONE
TALES OF EDUCATIONAL MALPRACTICE

The place of Passion in today's classroom

IN HIS VIDEO, "I JUST SUED THE SCHOOL SYSTEM," spoken word artist Prince EA, otherwise known as Richard Williams, argues that today's school system commits "educational malpractice" (Prince EA, 2016). This phrase succinctly encapsulates all of the ills that haunt the modern education system, not only in SSA, but also throughout the world. Prince EA also provides further inspiration for the first part of the book's title, "You Can't Make Fish Climb Trees," as he argues that this is exactly what the education system does to students by teaching them outside of the range of their natural abilities.

Prior to focusing solely in the education system in SSA, I feel that it is necessary to provide a general global context for all that is wrong with contemporary schooling. In this first chapter, I will provide two stories: the first comes from my Canadian colleague, Aviah, while the second recounts my own experience with the SSA school system. While it may seem that the first story deters from the focus on SSA, it actually complements the book in several ways. First, it illustrates that the educational ills in SSA constitute a type of global epidemic that stretches across the world, especially in today's globalized and multicultural reality. Secondly, it illustrates that the origin of SSA's flawed school system actually emanates from the European schooling system that served as the precursor to Canada's own education system, discussed in more detail throughout Chapter 2. This reality suggests that the Canadian and SSA school systems share the same poisonous roots; however, the case in SSA is much more drastic given the financial and resource limitations that prevent it from advancing further, as elaborated in Chapter 4 and 5. In fact, I introduce my colleague's story before mine to serve as a foil to my own experience. The reader will see how the educational inadequacies in the first story are clearly exacerbated in the second tale, the experience of SSA education.

In the two stories that follow, each of us experiences several negative effects from failed and ineffective school systems. These stories provide a legitimate context for the need to implement authentic learning by revealing the failures of the traditional, industrial mode, teacher-centered education system in Canada but more poignantly in SSA. The first story, which takes place in Ontario, shows how even the wealthy and developed countries still retain industrial-mode elementary and secondary schooling along with ineffective postsecondary education systems that fail to connect academia to the real world. The second story, which takes place in SSA, is where I recollect my encounters with schooling in Uganda. Despite differences in location and culture, both stories contain striking similarities to show that students around the world still experience the same flawed systems. I will begin with the story of my Canadian colleague, Aviah, who grew up in a relatively wealthy suburb of Toronto.

STORY 1: CANADIAN EXPERIENCE

Aviah recounted that from as early as she could remember, her parents had indoctrinated her to believe that a university education represented the key to success in life. All through the long years of high school, she recalled that her parents had reinforced this truism, convincing her that without marks in the high nineties, she would amount to nothing more than a homeless person, lucky to even pump gas.

In particular, Aviah relayed the words of her father during our interview: "He asked me if I wanted to work there for the rest of my life" (Aviah R., personal communication, August 20, 2017). She told me that those words still echoed in her ears, the words that he had spoken during one of the countless dinner conversations in which he had enlightened her with his wisdom. That was during the days when she was working overnight shifts at the Tim Horton's on the corner of her street, sitting groggily at the dinner table during what was technically her breakfast.

Aviah recalled that she had spent the majority of her primary and secondary school years just putting in the minimal effort required to get Bs and Cs. She explained that even as an elementary school student, she hadn't seen the point in many of the "cookie-cutter" lessons and worksheets that teachers force-fed students, resulting in her attention wandering to other things. She stated, "I remember one day in Grade 8, where I was walking behind another student and I saw that his T-shirt said something about a prisoner of war. And then it dawned on me, school was a prison. I was a prisoner" (Aviah R., personal communication, August 20, 2017).

When I asked her to elaborate further, she went on to explain how she felt stuck inside of a stuffy room all day and forced to perform tasks that the teacher wanted: "Copy this. Copy that. Be quiet. Be nice to others. There were so many rules" (Aviah R., personal communication, August 20, 2017).

And there were lines:

> All of the desks were lined up in neat rows, just like the way they expected you to do your cursive writing – within the lines they mandated. And you lined up to move from room to room, whether it was the gym, the library, or the music room. You lined up to go to recess. You lined up to come back in from recess. The lines took forever to get moving, and I often got fidgety, resulting in some form of discipline, usually detentions or writing yet more lines. It seemed that the punishment for being bad in school was just to experience more school. (Aviah R., personal communication, August 20, 2017)

She revealed that when she was six or seven, her parents took her to see a child psychologist. She barely remembered many details about this incident, but she does remember her parents mentioning this incident several times, often when they tried to convince her of how bright she was and how much potential she had. "You can do anything you want," her parents had often said. "Your IQ is off the charts" (Aviah R., personal communication, August 20, 2017).

She told me that one day the psychologist had been going on and on to her parents about how she could be anything from the President of the United States to a petty criminal. "Apparently, I had fallen asleep in his chair during this conversation, and I remember that my parents were none the too happy afterwards" (Aviah R., personal communication, August 20, 2017). Apparently, the psychologist had encouraged her parents to enroll her in a private school, which her parents believed would enable teachers to better reach her gifts. However, she told me that rather than seeing this possibility as an opportunity, she perceived the idea of private school as a threat, which, as she described, encouraged her to intentionally sabotage the entrance examinations. "I don't remember much of this, but apparently I aced the English test and left the math test completely blank. I don't know that I did this out of maliciousness, but that's what [my parents] told me had happened" (Aviah R., personal communication, August 20, 2017).

After failing to gain entrance to private school, Aviah continued her educational journey in public school. By her accounts, her behavior had worsened to the point where she had reached rock bottom: the dreaded strap.

> I forget what I had done, perhaps sneaking away from the school grounds with a group of other children to buy some candy at the nearest corner store. Of course, it was against school rules to go off school property during lunch hour, but we did it anyways [sic], knowing the potential consequences of being caught, which, of course, is exactly what happened. I remember the principal saying something about drastic measures for drastic situations before I received the strap. Up to that point, I, along with other children, had regarded the strap as some sort of urban legend, but there it was, hidden in some drawer in the principal's bureau. In a way, I had demystified the legend." (Aviah R., personal communication, August 20, 2017)

As I will recount in my upcoming story, receiving the strap was a common experience not only in Canadian schools, but also in SSA schools.

Aviah then proceeded to tell me that at some point, likely in junior high, when she was still playing pranks on teachers and neglecting her schoolwork, her father's words had finally sunk in.

> I don't remember the exact moment of epiphany, but I do remember that I devoted myself solely to the pursuit of my studies, earning those top marks throughout high school and receiving acceptance to all three universities to which I had applied. In order to get there, I had sacrificed everything: my social life, my hobbies, and my sports. (Aviah R., personal communication, August 20, 2017)

She explained that from this point, she gave every ounce of energy to her studies, even at the expense of reducing the hours she spent at her part-time job and jeopardizing her ability to save for university. She learned to adapt to what she called "the system," which entailed listening in class, taking meticulous notes, completing her homework, and memorizing information from her textbook (Aviah R., personal communication, August 20, 2017).

This part of the story has a happy ending of sorts, as her hard work had paid off and she had become accepted at all three universities to which she applied. She told me that when university started, she marveled at the beauty of the campus and the fact that she was now officially an adult. Although she felt like she had reached some sort of landmark, she knew that the journey was far from over. She recalled that:

> On the two-hour car ride from my childhood home to the university residence where I would be staying, my parents gave me "the talk" about avoiding the distractions that victimized many first-year students, including alcohol, drugs, and sex. They had nothing to worry about, as my sole focus involved my studies. (Aviah R., personal communication, August 20, 2017)

Her parents had prepared her for the hard work that university involved, so she wasn't surprised at the hundred-plus pages of reading that professors dished out after every lecture. What did surprise her, however, was the fact that her assignments, which had easily received high nineties in high school, had been marked anywhere from sixty-eight to seventy-five. She told me that she felt stunned: "All of those Saturday nights that I stayed in my dorm alone, awaiting the return of my roommates from wherever they had staggered off, to try to make sense of anything from Plato to Picasso, had gone for naught" (Aviah R., personal communication, August 20, 2017).

Once again, it was the words of her father that had motivated her. "You don't just work hard," he told her one day. "You work *smart*" (Aviah R., personal communication, August 20, 2017). Subsequently, she sought to learn the secrets of success at the university level, just as she had done at the secondary level. She explained that after every poor essay grade, or at least every grade that failed to meet her expectations, she sat down with her professors in their "musty, book-filled offices" and had them explain every grammar mistake to her. She arranged her classes in a way that would allow her the maximum the amount of study time and that allowed her to avoid early mornings, which she termed "the bane of [her] existence" (Aviah R., personal communication, August 20, 2017). Most importantly of all, however, she told me that she learned to get outside of her dorm and enjoy the real world from time to time.

She graduated with all of her marks above eighty and felt proud of herself. After she graduated, however, everything changed:

> after the pomp and splendor of my graduation ceremony was over and reality set in, doubt started to creep in. The day of my graduation had been beautiful; despite rain showers all week, the sun finally emerged for my ceremony. I had felt foolish adorned in the traditional cap and gown, almost as if I had reverted to my childhood and dressed up for Halloween. (Aviah R., personal communication, August 20, 2017)

She told me that when her name was called to receive that coveted piece of paper in front of everyone, "goosebumps broke out on my skin. This was everything that I'd ever worked for, not just for the past four years of slogging through paper after paper, but for my entire life" (Aviah R., personal communication, August 20, 2017). She recalled that her parents and younger sister had tightly enveloped her in a big family hug, which she said had made it even more worthwhile. "After years of pushing me every day, pushing me to get out of bed in time for the school bus, to finish my assignments before the deadline, to save my money for university, this was the finish line" (Aviah R., personal communication, August 20, 2017).

At least that was what she had hoped for. She recounted that night, she and her family had all gone out for dinner, where she "envisioned the brilliant future that the sun glinting off of [her] framed diploma had seemed to promise" (Aviah R., personal communication, August 20, 2017).

But then everything changed. As days went by, she waited for something to happen. As she told me, nothing did, and her parents began to wonder what was going on.

> There was no job waiting for me. No recruiters or headhunters were beating down my door, offering me the key to a Golden Office at the top of some Ivory Tower. I realized that it had all been a lie, some fairy tale I had imagined or even misinterpreted from the words of my parents. (Aviah R., personal communication, August 20, 2017)

With no other choice, she went back to the same job that she had worked at for the four years of university. "Somehow, despite my university degree, I found myself back at Tim Horton's working the night shift for what amounted to chump change. I felt defeated, as if everything I had ever believed had just been rendered meaningless." (Aviah R., personal communication, August 20, 2017)

From the moment that she returned to what she had considered a temporary stepping stone, she felt resentment for what life had dealt her, especially since she sensed backlash from some of the employees. "One of the employees, who was taking his business degree, asked me why I didn't have real job. He boasted about how his business degree was more useful, but then he just ended up working at Future Shop" (Aviah R., personal communication, August 20, 2017). She told me how offended and stung she felt, especially since she didn't have an answer to his question. In fact, she didn't actually know how to find what her insensitive coworker had termed a "real job." She explained:

> everything that I had considered doing for a living seemed to require either a different degree or postgraduate studies, which would mean even more money that I didn't have. Tim's paid me only a nickel above minimum and, since my parents charged me rent now that I had graduated, I would have to take at least a year off to save for tuition. That would also mean that I had to work a full sixteen months at Tim's, which I absolutely hated. (Aviah R., personal communication, August 20, 2017)

As I clearly sensed from the interview, she felt crushed that all of those summers she had worked at Tim Horton's and counted down to her graduation were merely an illusion, as she was still stuck working for nothing, which she describes as being "a mere peon at the bottom of the social hierarchy" (Aviah R., personal communication, August 20, 2017). She recounted that even her boss must have sensed her attitude and assigned her the worst possible jobs, including toilet duty and baseboard cleaning.

Aviah told me that she wanted to get out of Tim Horton's so badly that she had begun applying to other jobs, which merely consisted of other menial positions such as retail or clothing, "a step up in life, albeit a small one" (Aviah R., personal communication,

August 20, 2017). She recounted that her parents were continually harassing her to get out and find something better, especially since she griped constantly about her job and they had to endure her complaints. However, she explained that she hadn't experienced any success at the job hunt, which she admittedly despised to begin with. "I hated the idea of selling myself on some piece of paper. Hadn't my diploma done that?" (Aviah R., personal communication, August 20, 2017).

One day, she had seen an online ad for a customer service job with management potential. She explained that the position paid more than she currently made and the management job paid twice that. "Eagerly, I had called the number and arranged an interview just like that. I couldn't believe that it had been so easy! Maybe this is what I'd been missing all along!" (Aviah R., personal communication, August 20, 2017).

She told me that on the day of the interview, she dressed in her best clothes, which, at that time, had consisted of a plain white shirt frayed around the collar, grey dress pants, and scuffed black loafers. She recounted that the man who interviewed her, barely older than her, had asked her a few questions and then told her that based on her education, not only was she hired but she was also a management candidate. She recalled her feelings at this moment: "I felt overjoyed! My education was finally paying dividends! My parents would be thrilled! In fact, when I had returned home that evening and told them the news, they hugged me joyously. Everything in the world was right again" (Aviah R., personal communication, August 20, 2017).

But not for long. The next day, she attended her first "training session."

> My illusions were shattered as I realized that I would be selling vacuum cleaners door-to-door. I walked out in the middle of the session, feeling the wind and rain assail me on the way to the bus stop. I was back to square one, overeducated and underemployed. (Aviah R., personal communication, August 20, 2017)

At that point, with the encouragement of her parents, she realized that the solution to her dilemma ironically involved more education. But she had no idea what she wanted to study. She explained that she had a few ideas, but nothing concrete. She felt extremely frustrated that she had to go through the process of completing lengthy applications all over again.

> Each application entailed the rigmarole of writing personal statements, ordering and submitting transcripts, and obtaining letters of reference. And that didn't even count the application form itself, which was no less complex than a passport renewal. During my last year, I had applied to

> a few programs, including journalism, but I hadn't been accepted anywhere. So, it seemed like yet another waste of time. (Aviah R., personal communication, August 20, 2017)

She elaborated upon her sense of anguish at this point:

> I was absolutely devastated that the last four years had meant nothing in the grand scheme of things. All of the money for which I had busted my tail, completely wasted. All of my beliefs about reality had come crashing down like an elevator with its cables cut. I felt stunned, like a prisoner who had dreamed about freedom and suddenly realized that I had actually been freer in prison than in the real world. (Aviah R., personal communication, August 20, 2017)

When all had seemed lost, the turning point came when she received a phone call one morning. She recalled the story clearly:

> We still had one of those old rotary phones, yellow and stuck to the wall with a short, thick, curly cord. So, of course, I had no opportunity to look at the call display screen to see who it was. I was actually expecting to hear my boss tell me that so-and-so hadn't shown up and beg me to throw myself into my uniform and run to work. Obligingly, I always had, not necessarily because I actually cared about the greedy corporation that had more regard for donuts than it had for its employees, but because I wanted to make money, as little as it was. (Aviah R., personal communication, August 20, 2017)

But it wasn't her boss that had called. It was the Chair of Graduate Studies at McMaster University, telling her that she had been accepted into the Master of Arts Program. She told me that this invitation to continue her education had seemed like "some sort of destiny," as she had always felt most comfortable in the academic realm.

> I returned to work with renewed enthusiasm, counting down the days until I was finally back where I belonged: in school. I had even laughed as she received the traditional pie-in-the-face treatment as a sendoff for my last day of work. I was determined never to go back there. (Aviah R., personal communication, August 20, 2017)

Her master program represented yet another chapter in her life, but certainly not without its myriad of challenges. She elaborated on those challenges:

> Although my parents had always told me that I was brilliant, I felt like a minnow in a pond of sharks. These people were literally geniuses, talking about concepts and using language that completely befuddled me. Where did they learn this? How did I get here? Was I really that smart? Apparently not, since I'd been waitlisted and only received acceptance because somebody else had declined the spot. (Aviah R., personal communication, August 20, 2017)

However, she explained that it wasn't just the aptitude of those around her in the program. The amount of work was nothing short of what she called "insane." Like other graduate students, she only attended three classes for two hours a week, but for each class, she had to write assignments every week, including twenty-five-page papers at the end of each semester. She told me about a mishap concerning her last paper:

> The very last paper was due on the day that I had to move out of my residence. Just as I had done for many other assignments, I had stayed up all night to write this paper despite the fact that I would be lugging heavy furniture out of my dorm for the entirety of the next day. At around 5:30 am, I had attempted to print that paper off my old Hewlett-Packard inkjet printer. That dinosaur had nearly chugged out my entire assignment, when, to my chagrin, it stopped. Everything shut down. (Aviah R., personal communication, August 20, 2017)

She proceeded to recount the climax of this story:

> My printer was on the lowest shelf of the computer desk that my father had purchased. I was on my knees in front of the printer, literally begging for everything to be OK. Literally praying that my assignment was still there, as my sleep deprived brain had failed to remember whether I had saved it. Miraculously, it was there, and I had proceeded to the next chapter of my life. (Aviah R., personal communication, August 20, 2017)

Despite the happy ending to her printer story, she told me that during the course of her master's program, she had once again become disillusioned. She explained that "again, I faced that hard question: what did I want to be? What did I want to do for the rest of my life?" She stated that she had been thinking "within that narrow box," where she envisioned herself working what society had termed a "respectable career." (Aviah R., personal communication, August 20, 2017)

When I asked about her idea of what constituted a "respectable career," she elaborated that it was one that paid six figures and provided pensions and benefits.

> My hope that was if I'd kept going with my education, I'd eventually just find something that met my expectations and utilized my talents. My dream was always to be a writer, so I wanted to find something as close to that as possible. But time was running out. I was racking up a student debt that I didn't want to even think about, and I had no prospects outside of returning to the food service industry. (Aviah R., personal communication, August 20, 2017)

She told me that at that time, her current prospect was to one day land a job as a professor. But those dreams were shattered by late November of that year. A conversation with a Ph.D. student revealed the truth about the hard path to professorship. She learned that the Ph.D. program alone entailed another four years of education, while most students took six years or longer to complete their doctorate. "I would be close to thirty when I graduated! That was crazy! By that time, most people had families and made the big bucks at their high-powered jobs." (Aviah R., personal communication, August 20, 2017)

She continued recalling the conversation she had with the Ph.D. student:

> Not only that, he told me, but you didn't get tenure for at least seven years after you get your Ph.D., which would put me in the thirty-five to forty range. There was no way I wanted to make pennies until I was forty. I couldn't do this anymore. That wasn't working smart, as my father had said. (Aviah R., personal communication, August 20, 2017)

As she explained, a Ph.D. graduate without tenure was forced to take first-year classes and make as little as $10,000 per class for the entire year. Even two classes only netted $20,000, and, as my colleague revealed, the workload was so heavy that you often stayed up all night just to prepare for your classes.

She expounded on her reaction to this conversation: "The shock was devastating. I had already spent the past five years putting myself through school. I applied for my Ph.D., but only halfheartedly. My true feelings must have shown through the application as I was subsequently rejected" (Aviah R., personal communication, August 20, 2017).

As she had done before in these moments of crisis, she once again took a different direction; she applied for a Bachelor of Education at two different universities and received acceptance to both schools.

In the end, she had chosen to return to the university where she received her Bachelor of Arts. "In many ways, it felt like home: the same people, the same landscape, the same Gothic architecture that had constituted the setting for four years of my life. But it wasn't at all like returning to the promised land" (Aviah R., personal communication, August 20, 2017).

As was the case in her previous educational experiences, she once again suffered a hard reality check. "I learned many things during my Bachelor of Education. I learned theories about how children learn. I learned games and activities that teachers use to motivate children while still teaching them the curriculum. I learned about the curriculum itself" (Aviah R., personal communication, August 20, 2017).

But, as she explained, the real learning didn't start until her practicum. Every Friday, she had school observation day.

> On that first observation day when that I entered the school to which I had been assigned, a low-income school in the vicinity of a trailer park, I was instantly transported back in time. I once again felt like a student, but with everything shrunk down to some surreal miniature version. Everything was so small: the desks, the chairs, the blackboard, the hallways, even the teacher, who I towered over. In some odd way, I still expected to receive some sort of discipline for something unknown that I had done, although now I was the teacher and not the student. Fifteen years had passed since I left elementary school for junior high, but nothing had changed: nothing but me. (Aviah R., personal communication, August 20, 2017)

As I will illustrate later in the book, I experienced the same sense of déjà-vu when reading my daughter's description of primary school in Uganda, which, even today, bears a striking resemblance to my own school days.

Aviah elaborated that, like the case in her own elementary years, bells still sounded to demarcate the day into distinct periods of learning. At the end of each period, children lined up and were instructed to quietly pass from room to room. Throughout the duration of her practicum, she found herself increasingly wondering if the children were actually learning anything.

As she explained, one of the few things that changed was the increasing challenge of classroom management. "Classroom management? What was that? I hadn't learned about any such thing in my classes back at the university. Yet, somehow, we were supposed to already know about it" (Aviah R., personal communication, August 20, 2017). She elaborated upon her astonishment that student teachers were supposed to, without the aid of conventional disciplinary methods, magically coerce these children to behave and to listen in class. "If we failed to succeed at this endeavor, we would, much like the students that failed to memorize their lessons, receive a poor report card" (Aviah R., personal communication, August 20, 2017).

She became increasingly frustrated, not just at the disconnect between the in-class theory and her practicums, but at the state of education in general. One of the other student teachers who taught in the adjacent classroom, separated from her own classroom by only a thin barrier that failed to prevent noise from permeating throughout the entire pod, had left her a tearful message on the phone: she was quitting the program.

Aviah explained that earlier that day, two of the associate teachers had intentionally set her and the other student up for failure. She recounted that over the lunch period, some child had spilled something in the classroom, which required the janitors to lock the door and spend extra time cleaning. Of course, she and her fellow education student never found out what exactly had happened:

> All we knew is that we had sixty children to try to keep quiet in the hallway while other classes were in session. After an initial period of confusion, and looking around for our associates, who had disappeared into the classroom with the janitors, I decided to start asking the children math questions while my colleague stood beside me, meekly beseeching the children to lower their voices. (Aviah R., personal communication, August 20, 2017)

She explained that eventually, she and her colleague were allowed back into the classroom. However, as she recounted, that incident had forever scarred her. "I wasn't a quitter, so, even after our two associates had berated us for how we handled the incident, I stuck with it, even when I knew that I wasn't going to teach in the school system" (Aviah R., personal communication, August 20, 2017).

But it wasn't just that incident that had convinced her not to teach. As she revealed, she had realized that there were so many things wrong with education. Classes consisted of thirty children, nearly one-third of whom had some sort of special need, whether it was ESL or a learning disability. She felt that they were just being pushed along from year to year regardless of whether they could actually master the skills required at that particular grade level. She shuddered to think of high school graduates that couldn't even read or write. That's the way the system was heading.

And then there was the administrative rigmarole. Teachers had virtually no assistance with the special needs children, as the educational assistants only visited the classrooms for something like two hours a week. So, the classroom teacher had to somehow help the special needs students, manage behavior issues, which occurred constantly, *and* teach the curriculum. It seemed like a monumental task. On top of that, she learned that schools no longer supplied resources for their teachers, so, after many ten-hour days at the school and fighting an hour of traffic each evening, she and her colleagues made several trips to Scholar's Choice and Education Station despite their insufficient bank accounts.

Despite her complaints, she felt helpless to change things: "I remember having a conversation with one of my associate teachers after class. She had said something like 'that's just the way it is,' which, to me, seemed like a copout, as I felt deprived of a real explanation" (Aviah R., personal communication, August 20, 2017).

Once again, as she told me, she was stuck at a crossroads.

> I had decided that this was it, I wasn't going through for any more education; I was twenty-five and in debt. But I also balked at the idea of teaching in a classroom because there was no opportunity for these children to actually learn. In fact, it broke my heart to see a girl in grade three that couldn't even write her own name on her math test, tears spilling down her cheeks in frustration. That was when I decided that I wanted to tutor. (Aviah R., personal communication, August 20, 2017)

Some of the other education students had told her about tutoring, where they made three times what she had made at Tim Horton's. "At that point, my new dream was to start my own tutoring business. I envisioned myself in a downtown high-rise apartment, students ringing my buzzer to attend a scheduled appointment" (Aviah R., personal communication, August 20, 2017).

Although it started slowly and she initially needed to supplement her tutoring income with various fast-food and retail jobs for a few years, Aviah eventually built a large enough clientele base to focus solely on her business. While the money was good, she explained that the greater gain has been seeing students who faced huge obstacles in their lives overcome those obstacles to realize their dreams: dreams that the current education system merely quashes.

While Aviah's story provides a snapshot of a flawed Canadian school system, my own story shows that even the aspects of schooling that Aviah takes for granted and despised, I lacked in my Ugandan experience.

STORY 2: SSA EXPERIENCE

I was born, raised and educated in Uganda, where my parents fled from the ethnic violence in Rwanda in 1959. As members of the Tutsi population, my parents felt oppressed in Rwanda yet were accepted by the government of Uganda. Many Rwandan refugees lived in Uganda, and their children were accorded the opportunity to study in Uganda regardless of the quality of education. When I was growing up, many children struggled to complete primary school, and the vast majority of students failed to complete secondary school. Like many other children of Rwandan origin whose parents had sought refuge and lived in Uganda since the 1950s, my first experience of school was as a refugee student. The conditions were difficult.

However, my parents went far beyond their parental responsibility to ensure that displaced children acquired an education, regardless of the quality. Whether or not there was food to pack for lunch, money to pay for school fees, books, and other scholastic materials, my parents made sure that we acquired some form of education. They wanted us to continue learning despite the impoverished socio-economic situation that surrounded us. But even amidst the most devastating poverty I have ever faced or witnessed, the education system never improved for me and other refugee kids; school and the approach to both teaching and learning always represented another traumatizing burden that only added to the misery experienced by our lack of basic needs.

Between the ages of eight and twelve, I snuffed out the flame of my kerosene lamp at 10 pm on most weekdays. By that time, I would have spent two hours on my geography homework, memorizing the waterfalls of the world or committing the battles of Napoleon to memory. Most weekday mornings, I would feel my mother's hand urging me awake at 3 am. After stumbling out of bed, I would dress and gather my school belongings. If we were late, we would miss the other primary school students who waited for me at the trading center an hour away.

Although my father still slept, he would soon attend to the 127 milking cows for which my family cared. My father didn't care much for school. He'd finished Primary 4 in Rwanda before leaving school to work with his father's cattle. In his mind, he believed that I should drop out of school to help him care for the animals. My family eventually moved from the refugee camp to work on a farm, where the Ugandan owner allowed my mother to sell whatever milk was left over once the bellies of her children were full.

My mother had only finished Primary 2, but she didn't agree with my father's insistence that her youngest son should quit school to care for cows. Her older brother, my uncle, lived in Kampala, the capital city of Uganda, and drove a university school bus. He had finished his secondary school education, and his job surrounded him with the heady conversations of professors and students. He urged his siblings to prioritize their children's education over all else. My mother tried her best to follow his advice; however, like nearly all other children in the country, she could not afford to send me to nursery school. Likewise, I missed the entire first term of Primary 1 because we lacked the money to pay my school fees.

My mother made many sacrifices to achieve her brother's vision. Not only did she sell her chickens for my school tuition, but she also woke early to begin the day by walking through the bush with me towards the school, which was ten kilometers away. By this time, my older sisters and brother had moved to Kampala the capital of Uganda, where they lived with my uncle to attend school. For half an hour, my mother and I would walk in silence, broken only by the spontaneous call of a rooster. Our destination entailed a trading center, where I would meet with other children. Once gathered, the parents would wave goodbye as their children continued towards the school along dirt paths and over a makeshift log bridge at the Kyetinda River.

Normally, this river stayed low and flowed slowly; however, during the rainy season, the deluge would push its boundaries beyond the moorings of the bridge and sweep the logs away. As a result, the children who lacked the ability to swim turned back and went home. These children would not return to school until two or three months later, when the bridge could be re-secured. For the boys who could swim, including myself, we would strip down, carefully tie our books into the centre of our uniforms, and then secure the books and uniforms to our heads. Then, we would cross the river by riding pieces of driftwood across the expanse. The girls merely waved at us, their necessary modesty and the country's lack of infrastructure leaving them physically and academically behind. The students left in our group would arrive at the school, just in time for the start of class at 7 am. For those of us who were lucky to continue with school, despite these barriers, we received teaching that rarely translated into meaningful learning. Both teaching and learning were always grounded in the one-size-fits-all education system.

When I arrived at school, my days were filled with the teachers' droning dictations of a myriad of random facts that I would need to regurgitate on my year-end exams. Sometimes, when the teacher, who only possessed a basic education of her own, tired of speaking, the only audible sound was the scratching of chalk. With our heads bobbing up and down in acquiescence to the teacher and her facts, we scrambled to copy the words on the board.

Even on my very first day of school, my learning consisted of a series of lines and dots that required perfect repetition in my new exercise book. Having missed the entire first term, I sat on a mat that my mother had sent, and for the first time, sitting among 150 other students in my Primary 1 class, I faced a teacher. I marveled at the pencil that I held in one hand and the fresh pages of the exercise book in the other. The teacher drew strange, alien-like symbols on the chalkboard and instructed us to copy them in our book. Then, he told us that we had only a few minutes and informed us that he would be coming around to check our work.

I stared at him without comprehension. He was severe-looking man, holding a wooden stick that looked increasingly ominous as the seconds ticked away. A small girl next to me nudged me. "Write," she indicated, gesturing towards the pencil and paper. I shrugged. I had no idea how to write. I had never been to school. Although my parents could sign their names, they had not taught me the alphabet, nor did I have early reader materials, board books, or flash cards.

The teacher began walking around the room. The children who had failed to complete the assigned task were rapped sharply on the knuckles with the switch. At this point, I began to experience fear. Then, I felt a touch. I looked down to see the girl's hand directing my fingers to hold the pencil. Like a puppeteer, she moved my hand up and down, side to side, to draw lines that resembled those written on the blackboard.

Although the teacher had passed me without incident, the education system still managed to leave an imprint on my future. The forced uniformity expressed on that day continued for the next thirteen years of my schooling. The system lacked concern that I had never written words or sat in a classroom. My educational interests, needs, or barriers to learning did not matter. The system completely lacked the ability to adapt to the social, cultural, and economic needs of the children within it. The first school I attended, as well as the many that followed, provided my classmates and I with a one-size-fits-all classroom: one teacher, one textbook, and one pathway to learning.

As a child, I loved to care for animals, and I imagined myself one day owning a large farm. My mother had watched my growing interest in the business of raising animals, and, in Primary 4, she gave me a small amount of money and instructions to buy a male and a female rabbit. Then, my mother helped me to build a small hutch. In a little over a year, I had close to 350 rabbits. We ate some of the rabbits and I sold the others. In fact, my rabbits enabled me to fully pay for three terms of school. I also gave away pairs of rabbits to friends in the neighborhood, hoping to help them to create an income stream that would help their families and finance their schooling.

I introduced the idea of rabbit farming to the teacher, explaining that she could use the rabbits as an educational project to teach the children to raise their own animals. Since the rabbits had already allowed me to pay my tuition, I knew that other people and organizations, including the school, could make money.

The teacher deflated my enthusiasm, telling me sharply: "No, you cannot mix those things with school," she said. Then, she contacted my mother, telling her that "He needs to sell all the rabbits so he can concentrate in class." As a result of this conversation, I lost my product and returned to focusing on the unique processes of the timber industry in the soft wood forests of British Columbia, Canada. My sister would pay my tuition that term.

By Primary 7, many of the students with whom I had begun had since dropped out. Josephine, the little girl who helped me write my first words, left school to care for her dying mother. A couple of girls who accompanied me on our long walks to school stopped because no one at home encouraged them to make the trek to school. These girls experienced many barriers to education: early marriage, caregiving duties, and menstruation. Many of these girls lacked the ability to overcome such obstacles. The boys also faced challenges. Often, they were required to remain at home to tend animals. Without mothers like mine, these children bowed to the wishes and needs of their families.

For my good friend Saidi, health and finances forced him to quit school. Saidi was injured in a game of soccer, causing him to stay home from school for three months. Finally, doctors realized that his pancreas was failing, and his family sold six cows, almost everything that they owned, to save his pancreas. When he finally healed, they had no money for school. Unfortunately, Saidi was an example of a common trend in SSA: families often had to choose between health and education, forcing them to sacrifice the child's education.

Saidi was full of creativity and initiative. While I bobbed my head up and down, memorizing the provinces of China, he was inventing a handloom that could weave very fine garment linings, similar to those imported from China. One day, he asked me if I wanted to join him to take his fabric to the merchants in town. We left at five in the morning and arrived by early afternoon. In a very short time, we had sold all of the fabric. The money that I held in my hands was the equivalent of a full month's wages for my mother. As a result, I began to work with Saidi whenever I could. Some days I would attend classes, but other days I would skip school and veer away to his small shop. I loved the work and the money. The money, however, made my mother suspicious. One morning, she followed me. I started out towards school then doubled back to Saidi's shop. When she walked by the shop, I was already at work weaving.

"So, this is the place where you get money and waste your school time!" Her anger was intense. "You are ruining your future!" She marched me to school and explained my absences to the headmaster. In front of the entire school, the headmaster condemned my behavior: I had been skipping school to make money without my parents' permission. Then, I was caned. The stick whistled through the air, and, at my backside, the whistle became a snap that would echo twenty-five times through the silent hall.

No one had asked me what I had learned at the loom or the market about sales, exports, and the textile industry. Instead, I was sent to boarding school, where I was separated from my mother and from Saidi and his shop. As I memorized the details of the French Revolution of 1787 - 1799, Saidi's business would expand into a mechanized factory that made my friend wealthier than most university graduates in the country.

At the boarding school, my family continued to scrape together tuition, mostly thanks to my sisters who had married and started small businesses in the city. In Senior 3, I won a soccer scholarship that offered me freedom from worrying about finances. Although I loved playing soccer, I lacked the ability to make soccer a meaningful part of my education.

During Senior 5, I finally realized the capacity for teaching methods to make learning as interesting as soccer. When Mr. Luke Ddumba entered our history classroom, he made history by asking us, for the first time: "What do you want to learn?"

Subsequently, we produced learning goals. Instead of dictating the lessons, he facilitated discussions. Instead of rote memorization, he assigned projects that had us racing to the library to learn more. We taught each other in the classroom and made connections to the "bigger picture". It was from his classes in history and divinity that I would later draw inspiration when I faced my own classroom of students.

By Senior 5, I was looking ahead towards university. In Uganda, the students who score in the top 2000 across the country are awarded a full undergraduate scholarship. My friend Chris and I perceived the scholarship as one of our few options for obtaining a university degree. I desperately wanted to continue my education despite the impoverished one I had received, and Chris had felt the same way. Neither of our families could afford to pay tuition, and I knew that a soccer scholarship was far from certain. For the next two years, Chris and I would push each other towards the Holy Grail of a university scholarship. We would wake at 7 am for a full day of class. After napping from 5 - 7 pm, we would arise for supper. There was mandatory study hall from 8 – 10 pm, and, after this obligation, Chris and I would study into the night. Often, we would fall asleep exhausted at 2 or 3 am and begin the next day in only a few short hours.

Similar to the learning system, the grading system also lacked personalization. After each term, we would get our entire classes' results on a long list, allowing students to see their grade and standing. The national results of the final secondary exams were also presented in this format. Chris and I travelled together to Kampala to see the results of the Uganda Advanced Certificate Exam. The list of the top 2000 students in the country was posted at the Ministry of Education. As we entered the office building, named Crested Towers, the tallest building in the city at the time, we held our breath.

Both our names were there. I spotted my name neatly typed next to *105*.

It was one of the most exciting days of my life. Behind the euphoria, however, was a cloud of uncertainty. I thought of all my relatives, neighbors, and friends who never had the opportunity to finish primary school as well as those that had dropped out of secondary school. I had grown up with so many children: some already married, another rich, some dead, and many barely making a subsistence living. I was one of the lucky ones. Despite my hard work, I knew that others had worked just as hard and yet the system had failed to translate that work into success.

As a freshman at university, the dominant message persuaded us to work hard in order to obtain an excellent degree and a successful job. Our professors reinforced this dogma, constantly reminding us that a poor degree would result in a low-paying job. This type of thinking further confirmed that the one-size-fits-all education system teaches students to work for someone else rather than pursuing their own interests.

I don't recall if I expected anything to change in my learning environment; if so, I would have been sorely disappointed. In my Economics 100 class at Makerere University, over 1000 students attended the lecture of a single professor. He scrawled on the chalkboard and dictated microeconomics theory. Students spilled out of the lecture hall onto the lawn outside, where they cocked their ears towards the speakers that blasted dictation from open windows. The students wrote down all of the information from the professor and then regurgitated it on exams that looked like every other exam: facts and figures, with little context.

During the course of my undergraduate degree, I never interacted with a professor on a one-on-one basis. It was not until my Masters in Economic Policy Management at Makerere University, a program developed by the international community, that I would discover a host of professors with the personalized teaching methods of Mr. Ddumba, our best teacher, advisor, and coach in high school.

In 1996, my family had returned to Rwanda, and, upon graduating with a Bachelor of Arts in Economics, I followed them. At this point, I did not know what to do. Although I possessed a university degree, I actually had very few skills that I could use in the real world. I applied to attend a United Nations Development Program Conference in Kenya, where I believed that I could learn further skills in economic policy development. By the time I received confirmation of the funding to attend, I had only a couple of days to obtain a passport. I went to the passport office, where the receptionist informed me that the standard wait time was three weeks. If I had the money, which I did not, I could fast track the wait to three days.

"May I speak to your director?" I asked. "Perhaps if he understood my situation and the opportunity for me to receive better training, he could have the passport fast-tracked without a fee." She denied my request, and then the phone rang. As she turned to answer it, I bolted past her down the hallway. When she shouted at me to stop, I was already knocking on his door. The director was a serving military major and medical doctor, working as Director General of Immigration. He listened to my case. "Are you looking for a job?" he asked when I finished. I confirmed that I was. "Well, when you are back, please come back and see me."

My passport was ready that same day, and, after the conference, I returned as he instructed. He knew of thirty-two military officers who needed a history and economics teacher to help them upgrade and obtain their secondary school diploma. He asked me if I thought I could teach them. Although I did not know if I could achieve this task, I needed a job.

So, I became a teacher. With no training, I drew heavily from the teaching methods of Mr. Ddumba. My students were quick learners, and two years later, the class passed their secondary school exams and I was out of a job. However, the Army Chief of Staff had heard of me from a former student. The commander had a son who was recuperating at home and needed teachers to come to his house for the next few months. This reality demonstrated the hierarchical nature of the system, which adapted to these needs of the privileged while neglecting the needs of the underprivileged. So again, without a teaching degree, I became a teacher. I was determined that my students not only gain knowledge but also understand this information.

After my student returned to school, I found myself looking for work again. One of the military officers found me a job as a loans officer in a military bank. Then, another former student referred me for a job as an auditor in the Rwanda Revenue Authority (RRA), showing me that connections with the military can be very helpful in finding work. As they often say these days with regard to landing a job, it's not *what* you know, it's *who* you know.

As an economics graduate without an accounting education, I became an auditor. This personal experience lends evidence to the skills gap in which many SSA graduates work jobs in fields other than the ones in which they graduated. My supervisor trained me on the job, and I quickly learned about balance sheets, corporate tax policy, and tax loopholes. For three years, I worked at the RRA until I won a World Bank graduate scholarship to attend a unique Master's program at my former University. I was heading back to Uganda for a completely different education experience.

My graduate program was developed by a large group of international stakeholders within the World Bank Institute (WBI), African Capacity Building Foundation (ACBF), and Japanese International Corporation Agency (JICA). Only sixty-seven students from all over the world were accepted each year. This program intended to produce policy makers 'without borders', indicating the training of policy makers who could fit in any part of the world to research, evaluate policy, and make relevant policy recommendations. This program represented a "one-of-a-kind" initiative, with no other comparable program existing in all of Uganda.

In these classes, I was introduced to a personalized learning model and to dynamic teaching methods. I not only learned theory, but I also worked in internships in Rwanda,

Ethiopia, Japan, and London. For the second time in my life, I was asked about my learning goals.

When I graduated, I was one of the few Rwandese students who had studied economic policy development. I returned to the RRA, and when it came time to implement reform within the organization, I was seconded to the Commissioner General's Office to support the international consultant advising the RRA about reform and modernization strategy. The consultant soon left for a better offer in Burundi, and I remained in Rwanda to implement the strategies he developed. For the first time in my life, I felt equipped to creatively problem solve and draw from the experience of other Revenue Agencies around the world.

However, I would not remain with the organization to complete the reform, because, around this time, the Human Resources and Institutional Capacity Development Agency (HIDA), a government agency in charge of developing, coordinating, and implementing capacity building initiatives, was seeking a Senior Program Coordinator. Again, through my military connections, a person who subsequently continued becoming a mentor for me, I would be seconded to HIDA and never return to the RRA.

When I look back at my career, I know that so much of it was "luck, hard work and a wonderful mother who had a vision." Thanks to my schooling, I had many critical learning gaps that left me scrambling to acquire knowledge on the job. In Rwanda, especially, in the early 2000s, this situation was not particularly unique. Everyone was scrambling not only because of inadequate education, but also because of the tragedy of a genocide that annihilated almost a million people. Unfortunately, this represents one of the ways in which tragedy begets luck.

Although this story is twenty years old, the education system in SSA is virtually identical today. Consider, for example, my experience of animal husbandry: imagine what the students might have learned or built if the teacher had incorporated the rabbits in her lessons? How many other students might have finished school or been equipped to feed their families? What might have happened, if, in social studies, the students had studied business practices, or, if, in history, they had studied the shared humanity of Hutus and Tutsis in Rwanda? Imagine how history might have changed!

Summary and Reflection

While history's opportunities may be lost, many more opportunities remain, depending, of course, on the future of education. As shown above, the people in both stories eventually found success despite the inadequacies of the education system. However, they lost time and opportunity on their way to success, and in addition, not all students have been so lucky to eventually recover from the disastrous consequences of an outdated school system.

Although my own educational upbringing differs markedly from that of my colleague, Aviah, especially in terms of our location, educational journeys, and obstacles, our stories share several interesting similarities that point to the dire need for change in the schooling systems of both Canada and SSA. Since these two regions are otherwise very distinct in every other way, the striking likenesses between their education systems suggest the universal nature of such schooling flaws, especially given their common European origin, as discussed in the upcoming chapter.

The first poignant similarity between the two stories highlights the apparent pointlessness of many of the instructional techniques and educational activities at all levels of our respective educational journeys. Although both of our parents provided us with the encouragement and motivation to continue our educations as far as possible, they, along with us, lacked an understanding about the inefficiency of the systems. While the prologue of the book introduced the idea of mass-produced, industrial age education, both stories depicted many aspects of this teacher-centered mode of education. My colleague's recollection of her elementary school featured neat rows, repetitive activities such as cursive writing, and punitive measures as a way of enforcing student compliance. Similarly, I experienced the mechanical processes of copying letters, memorizing facts, and corporal discipline. In fact, discipline occurred frequently in my primary school, as, similar to Aviah receiving the strap in elementary school for leaving school property, I was caned for skipping school. At the level of higher education, both of us experienced solely the lecture mode of learning; while Aviah completed a practical component during her education degree, she attested to the complete lack of connection between the theory learned in her classes and the actual reality encountered in the schools. She told me that back at the university, her instructors lectured about child development theories and educational history, but when she was thrust into the classroom full of chaotic children, none of that mattered. I experienced a similarly chaotic atmosphere in my undergraduate economics classes, where hundreds of students crammed into a small lecture room to hear a professor recite theories to us, theories as seemingly meaningless and isolated from reality as the history of education was from a class of real children.

The second striking similarity in our stories, and perhaps the most remarkable, involved the enormous gap between academia and the labor market, leading to both of us initially becoming unemployed university graduates. Although Aviah pursued an undergraduate degree, a master's degree, and a professional education degree, she still struggled to obtain a job after any of her programs, eventually deciding to pursue her own business, a response in keeping with one of the major trends guiding the creative economy, discussed further in Chapter 6. Similarly, I graduated with an economics degree and lacked the ability find work in my industry; only after relentless efforts did I obtain a part-time, temporary teaching job in the military field. While both of our educational journeys ended in a positive fashion, with Aviah becoming a tutor and a professional writer, and me climbing the corporate hierarchy within the Rwandan government and eventually moving to Canada to work in a similar capacity, we both struggled to find a job in our field. Aviah initially resorted to working in fast food while growing her tutoring business, and I entered the field of teaching despite my economics degree. The fact that we both struggled to find jobs in our field, needed to find work outside of our intended industry, and took a while to establish our eventual niche highlights the growing deficiencies in the education systems of both of our counties. In addition, our common trajectories signify the vast chasm between the world of academia, where schools attempted to prepare students for a corporate job in a narrow, singular career, and the marketplace, where the prevalence of the creative economy blended industries, shuttled people from job to job, and encouraged entrepreneurship. The remainder of the book highlights the inability of outdated, industrial-era schools featuring teacher-centered learning methodologies to adapt to the contemporary creative economy, therefore suggesting that education undergo significant changes to adapt to reality, especially in SSA.

Despite the congruencies between the two stories, a comparison of the education system in Uganda with that in Canada illustrates that while Canada's schooling systems require some restructuring, the problems festering in SSA schools are much more extreme. While Ugandan education, as well as that in other SSA countries, still follows teacher-centered methods that isolate students from the real world, these schools also suffer from more extreme resource shortages that further impede the quality of teaching and learning, discussed in Chapters 4 and 5. As Chapter 4 highlights, the paucity of material, technological, financial, knowledge, and human capital prevents SSA education from adapting to the modern realities of the creative economy. Despite these problems, however, Chapter 5, which presents examples of authentic learning initiatives that have been successfully implemented in SSA countries, offers some hope that in spite of the obstacles facing these countries, they can overcome the barriers to consider the wholescale use of authentic learning methodologies at all levels of education.

While much of this book has been informed by academic research and personal interviews, it also draws upon popular culture to speak to the sad state of schooling. In particular, a few of the sources share my cultural roots, making the connection to Africa much more apparent. Two popular entertainers, Prince EA and Suli Breaks, speak candidly about the failings of the current education system. Prince EA discusses the inadequacies of contemporary education in his video "I Just Sued the School System." In this dramatic monologue, Williams argues that school systems have remained static since the Industrial Revolution when students were molded into future factory workers, taught not only isolated and meaningless facts but also indoctrinated with the characteristics of an obedient slave through the ability to adhere to rigid structures, follow instructions, remain quiet, obey authority, and comply with rules. Both of the people in the above stories experienced this type of system, forced to conceal their talents or hide their passion underneath the redundant bureaucracy known as modern education. Unfortunately, Williams' assessment is bang-on, and, an even sadder reality indicates that this system remains at the postsecondary and even graduate levels of education. As Williams states, educators have been concerned with "turning people into robots" and those who have higher aspirations, like the two people in the stories, endure considerable suffering with their talents squandered in a school system that remains completely alienated from reality.

Along with Williams, Suli Breaks concurs that the education system has lost relevance in the modern world. Specifically, he argues that society has progressed with advanced technology, such as the internet and mobile devices, yet schools remain hierarchically structured and rigid in their methods (Philby, 2013). Williams agrees with this assessment, providing visual evidence of his beliefs. In order to illustrate this point, Williams shows two pictures of phones and then two pictures of cars, each of which have changed substantially over a period of 150 years. However, the two pictures of the school system remain strikingly similar despite the passage of nearly two centuries. By remaining stagnant, education systems throughout the world have been destroying students through their inflexible approach to education. As Williams remarks, schools have been "killing creativity [and] individuality," thus demonstrating "intellectual abuse" and "educational malpractice" (Prince EA, 2016), the latter of which has inspired the title of this story. This educational malpractice has left many students frustrated, penniless, and jobless after a long hard road of education. Even the two survivors illustrated in the vignettes, both extremely bright and talented people from different parts of the world, were, to some extent, victimized by the "intellectual abuse" at the hands of the modern education system.

Another major issue brought to the forefront by both poets concerns the aspect of assessment. In particular, Suli Breaks strongly opposes the concept of assessing all students in the same manner and giving grades to students as a symbol of determining their worth (Philby, 2013). Since all students, as both poets point out, have different needs, interests, passions, and learning styles, they required different assessment methods that most accurately represent their learning in a particular class. Williams echoes Breaks' sentiments, describing the grading process as one that treats students like cattle, rating some students as "grade A" while rating others according to their achievement on a standardized "black and white" assessment (Philby, 2013). In his song, "I Will Not Let an Exam Result Decide My Fate," Breaks maintains that "the finals are never final ... because they never prepare for the biggest test, which is survival" (Philby, 2013). Ironically, the two stories that appear earlier in this chapter provide a reverse perspective on the inability of test grades to determine a person's future. Both of the people in the vignettes received top grades in their respective universities; however, neither person reaped the rewards of finding a lucrative job immediately following graduation. Conversely, as Philby (2013) points out, many students who drop out of school go on to become millionaires by starting their own businesses or inventing their own products, as illustrative of today's creative economy, discussed at length in Chapter 6. Hence, exam grades certainly do not determine a person's future.

Through their pertinent analogies, Williams and Breaks drastically illustrate the urgent need to modify the education system. Schools, which assess students by their ability to circle a correct answer on a standardized, multiple-choice test, are like people who "judge fish by their ability to climb trees" (Prince EA, 2016), resulting in students being labelled with learning disabilities. In the real world, people don't sit at desks and circle bubbles on a printout. People all have unique abilities that teachers, and the system that produces and trains teachers, need to harness in order to help students recognize their strengths, develop those strengths, and market them in the real world. Both of the people in the preceding stories were, at least initially, deprived of the opportunity to market their skills and needed to take unconventional detours in order to achieve their goals. As Williams states, the world has changed, and it no longer requires students to sit quietly at a desk and copy notes to memorize for a test. It requires the necessary skills to succeed in today's creative economy – innovation, collaboration, critical thinking – and many others that the remainder of this book, especially Chapter 6, will elaborate upon.

The remainder of this book discusses the desperate need to change the education system and proposes authentic learning as a cure for this malady, beginning with the history of education in Chapter 2. After situating the various educational philosophies in the appropriate historical context, Chapter 3 explains the student-centered learning method of authentic learning, which forms the theoretical basis of this book. Next, Chapter 4 introduces the state of education in SSA before discussing the conditions for the introduction of authentic learning in SSA in Chapter 5. Chapter 6 introduces the concept of the creative economy as well as the way in which this new paradigm affects both schools and society. Subsequently, Chapter 7 outlines the benefits of authentic learning, especially within the context of the creative economy, to the different stakeholders identified in the prologue of this book. The final chapter, Chapter 8, presents the factors preventing the implementation of authentic learning in SSA and suggests strategies for overcoming these barriers.

CHAPTER TWO
HISTORY OF EDUCATIONAL PHILOSOPHY

Learning by Observation and Practice

THE TWO STORIES FROM THE INTRODUCTORY CHAPTER demonstrate that the education system remains in dire need of change. In order to understand how the education system reached the point of malfunction and stagnation discussed in the opening chapter, it is useful to begin with a history of education along with educational philosophies that accompanied that history. Briefly speaking, an educational philosophy is "the philosophical study of education and its problems" (Noddings, 1995, p. 1). The last word in this definition, "problems," indicates the imperfect nature of the education system that exists throughout the world. Although the main focus of the book remains on SSA schooling, this broad survey of educational history will provide the historical and geographical context for the student-centered philosophy of authentic learning as well as the focus on African education.

INDIGENOUS EDUCATION

Before the implementation of formalized schooling throughout the world, most hunter-gatherer societies transmitted knowledge directly from parent to child. Keep in mind that in these societies, any learning occurred orally due to the lack of written literacy; in fact, the printing press, which wasn't invented until the Middle Ages, represented the precursor to today's formal education system, which will be discussed later in the chapter.

These hunter-gatherer societies lacked a distinct educational philosophy apart from the need for parents, grandparents, or other adults to teach their children, as well as for other children in the group to gain practical knowledge of real-life tasks. In many societies, in fact, children instigated their own learning through independent explorations of nature and by observing adults perform the basic tasks required to survive. Some of these duties included building a hut, making a fire, preparing a group move, taking care of children, hunting, gathering food, and caring for the sick (Gray, 2008). After observing adults, children incorporated these essential duties into their play or even helped adults in these chores. In addition, children also acquired knowledge from cultural rituals that involved the transmission of knowledge from one generation to the next. Such rituals included music, art, games, dances, and oral storytelling (Gray, 2008).

As children matured, they gradually became more adept at the necessary skills by performing parts of the duties on their own with limited supervision and feedback from parents or other adults in the nomadic group (Gray, 2008). This method of self-initiated learning, in many ways, resembles authentic learning through its independent exploration, limited facilitation, and practical nature. Unfortunately, a large gap of time remains between this seemingly authentic indigenous way of learning and the relatively recent invention of authentic learning as a student-centered method of education. The path from what was considered 'primitive' learning to formal education shows that things do not always improve over time. This demonstrates that while human needs have evolved beyond seeking food and shelter, the education system has failed to fully and adequately address those needs.

Although the main focus of the book remains on SSA, it is worth briefly discussing the Canadian history of education as a means of comparison to Indigenous African education, especially since both countries, despite their differences, bear a startling resemblance to one other in terms of educational history. In Canada, Indigenous children learned in practical and culturally-appropriate ways that contradicted the formalized education later introduced by colonizers. Borrows (2009) states that Indigenous knowledge, and, by extension, Indigenous law, consists of five ways of knowing: sacred, natural, deliberative, customary, and positivistic. All of these principles underline the importance of the Indigenous Creator and the creation as well as emphasize respect for and harmony with the land. First, sacred knowledge originates from the Creator and manifests in creation stories transmitted throughout the generations; these imperatives detail the necessary function or role that each individual and creature fulfills within the universe. Natural knowledge entails an examination of the natural world, including relationships among animals, plants, and humans as well as a consideration of the landscape and its resources. Furthermore, deliberative knowledge refers to the human interpretation of laws in the context of negotiations and discussion, such as band councils. Positivistic knowledge constitutes the formation of laws into systems of rules that govern the way in which humans relate to nature. Finally, customary knowledge and laws develop through established modes of behavior and include social norms that reflect the underlying values of a community (Borrows, 2009). These ways of knowing demonstrate that the education system to which Indigenous children are exposed must match their cultural models. However, with the introduction of formalized schooling, marked by the tragedy of residential schools, many Indigenous children have lost touch with their cultural, linguistic, and spiritual roots.

Similar to Indigenous Africans, Indigenous Canadians take a holistic perspective in both life and education; they learn most effectively when understanding the connection between all aspects of situation, especially as they relate to the Creator (Fulford, 2007).

These cultural theories permeated early Indigenous education; Wells (2015) reveals that prior to colonization, Canadian Aboriginal communities educated their youth through practical means such as demonstrations, collaborative learning, ritual participation, skill development, and oral teaching, which transmitted cultural traditions, knowledge, and tasks relevant to society (Wells, 2015). Since this time, however, the onset of residential schooling, which separated students from their parents and forced them to learn English and Christianity, eradicated Aboriginal culture and resulted in a plethora of social problems, including unemployment, substance abuse, poverty, illness, and mental health problems (Dion, Cantinotti, Ross, and Collin-Vezina, 2015). Not only were Aboriginal children torn from their parents and placed in boarding schools, but they also endured abuse from the religious teachers, who indoctrinated them into Christianity while suppressing their native languages and worship practices. While my story shares similarities with residential schooling, as my mother forced me to attend boarding school and I, like Aboriginal children, experienced a colonially-imposed, teacher-centered schooling system, the calamity that befell these Aboriginal children makes my situation pale in comparison.

Along with the recent reconciliation attempts in Canadian society, Aboriginal education has experienced a renewal of sorts, an attempt to overcome the negative effects of residential schooling by returning to prior Indigenous methods of education. For example, Yellowhead Tribal College (YTC), an Indigenous postsecondary institution in Alberta, recaptures traditional Aboriginal culture through its educational content and methods. Not only does this unique postsecondary education institution provide Indigenous content, including Cree language, Indigenous history, and Aboriginal governance, but it also takes a holistic approach to nurturing students through Aboriginal teaching methods and providing cultural exposure. Students can learn cultural traditions, practice Aboriginal spirituality, and consult with elders alongside their studies. (YTC, 2017). Despite the innovation inherent in this approach, YTC represents only one of a few Indigenous postsecondary institutions in Canada, and the only one in Edmonton. Nevertheless, this institution, and other similar initiatives, show that, at least in Canada, the return to Indigenous ways of knowing is underway. This initiative is accompanied by the development of life skills relevant to gaining and regaining meaningful knowledge and employment in contemporary society.

Indigenous African Education

Similar to Indigenous Canadian societies, their SSA counterparts educated children with culturally-appropriate learning methods that transitioned students smoothly from their education to their adult working lives. While the predominant social viewpoint maintains that African countries lacked adequate education and training systems prior to the implementation of western school systems, Indigenous societies throughout Africa strongly resembled Canadian Aboriginal society prior to colonization and residential schools. The earliest forms of education in Africa, known as Indigenous African Education (IAE), provided students with preparation for a professional or occupational activity or task within their community (Majoni & Chinyanganya, 2014). Ndofirepi and Ndofirepi (2012) state that IAE "is unlike formal western education in that it is very practical and pragmatic and prepares the individual for life passing on the values of life that have been evolved from experience and tested in the continuing process of living" (p. 19). African children and adolescents learned both survival and occupational skills that enabled them to function within society (Mosweunyane, 2013). Resembling a type of apprenticeship, IAE taught students aspects of a trade, such as farming, hunting, carpentry, medicine, spirituality, dressing, cooking, and metallurgy. One Ugandan university professor recounted that "if you were to become a blacksmith, you would work with this person and produce an item" (N. Itaaga, personal communication, April 20, 2017). The concept of "producing an item" relates directly to Steve Revington's definition of authentic learning, which requires that such learning produces "a tangible outcome" (Revington, 2016). From this perspective, IAE resembled authentic learning in its objective of producing a product.

In addition to the practical and real-world nature of IAE, this type of education related to authentic learning through the fact that the teachers, elders, parents, or grandparents, served as facilitators rather than direct instructors. The concept of the facilitator or mentor concurs with Steve Revington's (2016) definition of authentic learning, where the teacher acts as "an event manager" rather than a dictator. One professor told me that that he learned various skills from his grandfather, including hunting and bark-cloth making (M. B. Mulumba, personal communication, April 20, 2017). Rather than providing direct instruction about useless and fragmented information, students learned practical skills that they needed for both their profession and lifestyle. For instance, children learned about practical tasks and aspects of life, including marriage counselling, money management, ethics, hygiene, and leadership training (Adeyemi & Adeyinka, 2002). Another professor from Uganda's Makerere University highlights the importance of problem-solving in IAE, which subsequently enabled people to deal with the problems or challenges that they faced in the real world (S. W. Wafula, personal communication,

April 20, 2017). Part of this practical training involved the concept of Ubuntu, or social etiquette, which teaches children values and beliefs, such as honesty, wisdom, solidarity, humility, courage, fortitude, morality, and respect for elders, as well as how to interact in certain social situations (Ndofirepi & Ndofirepi, 2012). As noted in Chapter 6, which explores the role of the creative economy in education, many of the skills that were implemented in IAE, including collaboration, leadership, problem-solving, and creativity, are sorely lacking from today's education systems, especially at the postsecondary level. From this perspective, the implementation of some IAE elements into the schooling of African children and adolescents will align more effectively with the labour market.

Similar to the way in which Canadian Aboriginals underlined five Indigenous ways of knowledge that promoted a holistic version of education, IAE consisted of five principles: preparationism, functionalism, communalism, perennialism, and holisticism (Adeyemi & Adeyinka, 2002). Preparationism aims to ready each community member to fulfill his/her destined role, while functionalism emphasizes pragmatism and the completion of practical tasks. Whereas communalism enhances the bonds among group members and emphasizes cohesion rather than competition, perennialism transmits cultural, linguistic, and religious traditions from generation to generation. Finally, holisticism creates a well-rounded individual through education in all domains, including cultural, economic, and political (Mwinzi, 2015). In fact, the principle of holisticism supported the learning of all aspects associated with a particular trade; for example, students learning the hunting trade learned about animal care, tool building, hunting techniques, methods for cleaning a carcass, and ways of selling the meat. Similarly, when Indigenous youth learned to build a house, they actually covered many subject areas at once, including geometry, physics, and geography (Adeyemi & Adeyinka, 2002). In discussing this holistic approach of Indigenous education, one Ugandan university professor described the learning approach in which students prepared for life as a hunter:

> Once students learned a skill, like for instance how to hunt, they would not stop there; they would learn how to treat the dog and how to slaughter the animal. In addition, students learned how to get to the market for the meat and make something useful out of the skin. (C. Mugimu, personal communication, April 28, 2017).

As is the case in housebuilding, hunting, as well as any other trade, involved more than a single skill, subject area, or even series of random facts, which today's education system seems to assume that students require for career preparation. Thus, this holistic approach to education allowed a student to prepare fully for their future trade without any extraneous or abstract information that they wouldn't use in their future lives. Similar to the case with Canadian Aboriginal children, Indigenous Africans placed great importance on the aspect of spirituality, which involved a mystical component that emphasized the ability of special community members to communicate with deceased ancestors (Mosweunyane, 2013), yet another practical aspect of a person's life. Although Indigenous African spirituality, especially to western audiences, may seem impractical, it emphasizes the holisticism underlying IAE as well as the important aspect of community, which ultimately connects education to the real world.

The IAE approach differs from contemporary education, which, as mentioned, compartmentalizes subject areas into distinct categories. This division of curricular content isolates children from the daily aspects of life, occupations, and their community (Majoni & Chinyanganya, 2014). Furthermore, unlike formalized education, IAE emphasized physical participation and practical tasks rather than theoretical knowledge; in other words, IAE was all about "doing" rather than "knowing." For instance, Indigenous African children learned and practiced rituals, music, dancing, art, role play, and oral literature (Majoni & Chinyanganya, 2014). The education that children learned from IAE pertained to their world rather than to a foreign world. Conversely, African children who received their education in colonial, European-style schools learned about geography and history from the perspective of their colonists rather than from their own land. One of the professors in my study explained that:

> For a child in Uganda, the sun rises every day at 6 am and sets at 7 pm in the evening. However, you are telling him that during winter, the sun rises at midday and by 4 pm, it is already dark. That is outside the imagination of this child. (N. Itaaga, personal communication, April 20, 2017).

By learning about a foreign world rather than their own, African children remain isolated from the reality that will not only help them to obtain a job but also function as an adult in their society.

In contrast to colonial education, IAE provides students with information about the landscapes and economies in the countries where they live. For example, the Karamojongs, a contemporary farming society, not only learn about farming methods but also have their schooling hours tailored around their agricultural responsibilities, thus allowing them to obtain a relevant and practical education while still pursuing their work (N. Itaaga, personal communication, April 20, 2017). As a result of their Indigenous education, African society was self-sustaining. They ran their own businesses and provided for themselves from the bounty of the land (C. Ssempala, personal communication, April 25, 2017). However, once the colonizers took over, these ruling elite destroyed the independence of Africans and forced them into dependence and slavery, concealing the roots of Indigenous local knowledge. Although SSA nations are now physically independent, they have lost touch with their cultural heritage; one professor stated that the "western influence from the western world … has concealed our indigenous knowledge" (P. Ssenkusu, personal communication, April 20, 2017) and another instructor stated that this influence has "eroded our minds" (S. W. Wafula, personal communication, April 20, 2017). Therefore, Indigenous knowledge and education differed substantially from the ideologies and methods of learning imposed by western cultures in the name of progress or modernity. Subsequent chapters suggest a return to some of the principles embraced in IAE as a more practical way of addressing the needs of the contemporary creative economy and filling needed skills gaps in the labor market.

After the full-scale development of agriculture, hunter-gatherer societies were replaced by agrarian societies, which eventually led to the development of formal schooling. The transition between Indigenous modes of learning and formalized schooling occurred at different times throughout the world. In Africa, missionaries from different parts of Europe and North America first began colonizing Africa in the fifteenth century, replacing IAE with a version of contemporary schooling that taught literacy to African children (Adeyemi & Adeyinka, 2002); this process reflected the compulsory residential schooling administered to Aboriginal Canadians. Accordingly, the remainder of this chapter will focus on the educational philosophies that defined formal schooling, which first began with the implementation of teacher-centered learning.

FORMAL EDUCATION

Teacher-Centered Learning

Within the context of educational philosophies, one major way of classifying the various learning ideologies concerns the difference between teacher-centered and student-centered education. The term "teacher-centered learning" may confound many people, even those who have spent several years within the education industry; these people may marvel at the use of the term, since it may seem obvious that learning should start with the teacher. Accordingly, teacher-centered learning involves philosophies that posit the teacher as the sole source of wisdom and knowledge and students as passive receptacles of learning. Various metaphors, including the ancient Eastern tea ceremony, where the master, depicted as a teapot, fills the student, a teacup, with tea in the form of knowledge, have been associated with this mode of education (Lewis, 2008). Within this framework, teachers provide students with direct content instruction, require that students memorize isolated theoretical facts, and assess students by means of standardized examinations, such as the multiple-choice format (Vavrus, Thomas, & Bartlett, 2011). As illustrated in the two tales of education gone wrong, both students were exposed to the teacher-centered learning method of education throughout their educational tenure, including even university. Both aspiring scholars were bombarded by books, pencils, papers, and blackboards; information fed from stern, knuckle-rapping teachers; isolated, boring facts required for memorization and subsequent regurgitation on standardized tests; a plethora of meaningless administrative and bureaucratic rules; and the expectation of going to college with a ready-made job waiting upon graduation.

Unfortunately, teacher-centered learning remains the centerpiece of a failed education system. Steve Revington (2016), concurring with Prince EA and Suli Breaks, maintains that the teacher-centered style of teaching and learning originated from the industrial era, where students learn passive obedience in the form of sitting quietly, taking their turns, and following instructions. Although this educational approach, which researchers have termed "mass produced education" (Robinson, 2010), responded to the needs of society during this industrial era, this style persisted despite the decline of manufacturing era (Revington, 2016). Ken Robinson (2010), in his video "Bring on the learning revolution," discusses the need to evolve beyond the current education system, which decades or even centuries of educators have conceived in the model of linearity. Education, according to Robinson, has always assumed that all students progress in the same linear track from kindergarten to university, which pushes them, like objects in an assembly line, from one point to another until they graduate, ostensibly ready for the world of work. This sense of pushing students along a continuously moving track was no more apparent than in the practice teaching experience of the Canadian colleague, who witnessed third grade children struggling to make sense out of written words on a page. Presumably, they would enter fourth grade with little progress before proceeding throughout elementary school, junior high, and high school with little learning beyond the bare basics of literacy and numeracy. And keep in mind, this story occurred in Canada, not in SSA, which witnessed even more dire circumstances. Although some parts of the world, including western countries, have taken strides to move away from teacher-centered learning, Robinson (2010) insists that such strides are largely insufficient, like the attempt to cut the diseased branches from a tree rather than ripping out the roots.

In order to discern the roots of teacher-centered learning philosophies, it is best to begin with the emergence of educational philosophies in general. Educational philosophies emerged along with the origin of philosophy in Ancient Greece. It's hard to imagine sandaled scholars in white robes walking throughout the agora of Athens, spouting dictums about how students should learn. However, this part of the story highlights the *beginning* of educational philosophies rather than the execution of fully developed and complex concepts. Plato, the original philosopher, argued that the objective of education included justice, fairness, and democracy from the perspective of both the individual and society. In this sense, Plato maintained that education enabled students to acquire complete knowledge of themselves along with an understanding of their function in the world. Plato believed that once students graduated from school, they had the capacity to contribute to a harmonious society that achieved its democratic goals through equality and fair competition (Lee, 1994). The main method by which Plato proposed that students acquired knowledge, currently known as Socratic questioning, interestingly contains some features of authentic learning. This method, which involves a continual series of questions designed to guide the learner towards some sort of discovery or truth about self, others, complex concepts, or society, represents a learner-centered approach where, rather than feeding a student the answer or providing with direction, the questioner helps the student to acquire the answer on their own. In this sense, the questioner, a teacher, instructor, therapist or another individual, acts as a facilitator rather than a dictator (Revington, 2016). However, some uses of Socratic questioning intentionally guide the learner towards a specific answer rather than allowing them to derive their own solution, thus resembling conventional, teacher-centered learning (Padesky, 1993).

Similar to Plato, Aristotle believed that the purpose of education involved strengthening an individual's concept of morality so that each person eventually became a good and virtuous citizen within a just society. However, while Plato believed that teachers should help students to arrive at the answer through the method of questioning, Aristotle perceived the teacher's role as instructing students directly on knowledge, reason, and morality. In this sense, education, or at least the teacher's role in it, seemed to move away from the concept of the student as the center of the learning experience. Based on Aristotle's belief that teachers can imbue students with habits, which constitute forms of behavior enforced through repetition, Aristotle's educational philosophy seems to imply that teachers must instruct students through the method of repetitive learning and influence them to acquire certain learnings chosen by society rather than by the student's own personal interests (Hummel, 1999). Strangely enough, although Aristotle succeeded Plato, Plato's philosophy seemingly contains elements of student-centered learning while Aristotle's philosophy apparently resembles teacher-directed learning. At the same time, however, Aristotle advocated for instructional strategies that support student-centered learning, including questioning, critical thinking, and active learning (Hummel, 1999). Based on the differences between the two philosophers, it seems that each man's educational beliefs contained aspects of both teacher-centered and student-centered learning, showing that the development of educational philosophies, were, to some extent, at a type of crossroads.

Let us now move forward to the Middle Ages. During the Medieval era, religion became paramount in all aspects of society, including education. The church rose in prominence, and through the establishment of church-run schools taught by religious leaders, controlled education. The objective of education in the Middle Ages involved teaching students supposedly universal maxims that sought to instruct students about morality and ethical decisions that enhanced their ability to achieve salvation and become reunited with God on earth and in heaven (Guisepi, 2007). Based on this viewpoint, education aimed to inculcate students with the moral beliefs inherent in society. Thomas Aquinas, among other philosophers of the time, perceived education as constituting part of Christian theology. His educational philosophy, termed Scholasticism, posited that God represented the only source of true, objective knowledge and that divine intervention provided people with an understanding of the ideological and moral truths (Galgonovicz, 2000). In this sense, the role of education entailed providing students with the tools to achieve unification with God, and, by this means, to gain ultimate knowledge. As a vehicle of God, the teacher represented the diviner of information, teaching students a set of single, objective truths about the way in which the world operates. Although Aquinas, unlike his predecessors, rejected repetition as a teaching strategy, he still emphasized book-based learning and memorization as essential to effective education (Galgonivicz, 2000).

Outside of the western world, ancient Eastern educational philosophies, despite their ideological differences from the west, maintained that religious indoctrination represented the sole aim of education. As was the case in the western world, Medieval Islam witnessed the transformation from individual tuition to formalized education within a classroom setting. Previously, children in the east acquired fundamental knowledge through direct parental education, apprenticeship in trades, or, for wealthier children, private tutoring from a renowned teacher. Educators believed that classrooms provided children with enhanced learning advantages through the facilitation of competition amongst peers, group discussions, and debates (Rizvi, 2006). Interestingly, some of these strategies reflect the student-centered learning methods associated with authentic learning principles. In addition, the famous concept of the "tabula rasa" or "blank slate," credited to western educationalist John Locke, actually emanated from one of the famous eastern philosophers, Abu Ali al-Husayn Ibn Sina, otherwise known as Avicenna. Avicenna argued that when children are born, they lack any prior knowledge; this theory disputed previous claims that individuals possessed prior knowledge of certain truths or understandings, such as that espoused by Plato. The concept of the blank slate implied that children gain knowledge only through their experiences in the real world, which allows them to comprehend abstract concepts (Rizvi, 2006). This revolutionary idea eventually gave rise to subsequent philosophies of education that placed the student at the center of the learning experience.

However, the Renaissance period witnessed a return to previous educational philosophies from the ancient Greek and Roman eras. During this more secular timeframe, the goal of education involved students for a particular social occupation (Guisepi, 2007), which seems to coincide with the objectives of Indigenous education, and later, student-centered or authentic learning. A famous Renaissance philosopher, John Milton, bridged the medieval and neoclassical educational ideologies by proposing that education serve a dual purpose: to link students to the ultimate truths of God and to create moral citizens that serve a function within a cohesive society (Murphy, 2007). Hence, Milton's objectives of education reflect the aims of both the religious medieval society and the more secular Renaissance era, which, in many ways, resembled the ancient Greek philosophies of education. Milton's belief that man intrinsically possesses imperfect knowledge of the world, and, through education, will refine this knowledge into more complete truths (Murphy, 2007), incorporates elements of both the Platonic theory of forms and Christian understandings of man's inherently fallen nature.

Moving slightly forward in time, John Locke enhanced Avicenna's concept of the tabula rasa in his own theory of education. Specifically, Locke envisioned the teacher as the source of ultimate wisdom and the student as the passive recipient of this vital knowledge. From this perspective, the objective of education purported to directly transmit information about truths from teacher to student (Englemann & Carmine, 2011). The role of the teacher served as the source of wisdom designed to inculcate students with objective principles, thus meshing with teacher-centered learning theories. In other respects, however, Locke's theories contained some ideals of student-centered learning, especially his suggestion that teachers encourage students to demonstrate critical thinking processes. Similar to later educational philosophies, Locke first proposed that teachers should facilitate student learning by relating new knowledge with previously-learned concepts (Locke, 1764). This idea provided the foundation for constructivism, the broad educational theory that suggested linking prior learning with new ideas. While some of Locke's concepts paved the way for the emergence of student-centered learning theories, including constructivism and eventually authentic learning, most of his philosophy remained firmly implanted within the orientation of teacher-centered learning. In addition to Locke's belief that teachers transmit objective knowledge directly to students, he also conceived student learning in a homogenous manner that treated all students as uniform entities (Locke, 1764).

John Stuart Mill expanded Locke's concept of the tabula rasa or blank slate to suggest that the inherent tendency of individuals towards logic and reasoning (Engelmann & Carnine, 2011), which corresponds with the classical philosophies of Plato and Aristotle as well as Locke's notion of developing critical thinking abilities in students. In addition to echoing some of the concepts espoused by previous thinkers, Locke supported the notion of educational reform that provided students with freedom by separating them from the uneducated masses of society. Mill's binary between reason and passion not only promulgated Platonic ideologies but also articulated the role of education in society: to foster reason and maintain its supremacy over emotions by encouraging students to subordinate their natural impulses to logical reasoning (West, 1965). Furthermore, Mill supported the advancement of Locke's ideas by conveying a homogenous approach to student learning that neglects individual differences among students. Although Mill and Locke still remained firmly within the tradition of teacher-centered learning, certain aspects of their theories, such as the idea of scaffolding and the importance of critical thinking or reasoning, contained some hope for the emergence of student-centered learning.

Student-Centered Learning

In contrast to teacher-centered learning, student-centered learning places the student at the center of the educational experience. The transition from student-centered to teacher-centered philosophies of learning represented a gradual evolution rather than an abrupt transition, as discussed throughout this chapter; however, for the purposes of contrasting the elements of their theories, most parts of this book treat the two pedagogies as distinctive styles. In fact, as many educators and entertainers referenced throughout this book maintain, most of the school systems throughout the world remain mired in systems that revolve around teacher-centered learning, with small changes only beginning to occur, mainly in developed countries.

While most of the previous philosophers maintained a teacher-focused approach to education, some of their ideas provided a strong foundation for subsequent theories that shifted the orientation of educational methodologies from the teacher to the student. The transition towards a student-centered approach to education began with Jean-Jacques Rousseau. Some of Rousseau's beliefs coincided with those of prior thinkers, including John Milton. Specifically, Rousseau, like Milton, believed that due to original sin, people existed in a state of sin. However, Rousseau differed from his predecessors in his belief that children possess a natural state of curiosity (Doyle & Smith, 2007); these beliefs echo the ideas behind Indigenous education as discussed in the earlier part of the chapter, thus suggesting that teachers encourage children to explore their environment as a means of acquiring information. Rousseau argued that since school systems inhibited student learning by suppressing the natural curiosity of the student, students should learn outside of the institutional environment defined by school walls. Furthermore, Rousseau criticized formal schools for harming the natural learning process by providing students with abstract concepts alienated from their natural experience, thus echoing the much more modern sentiments expressed in the previous chapter. In order to reverse this damage, Rousseau proposed that learning begin with environmental exploration that identifies student interests before relating these aspects to formal concepts. Despite his belief that teachers should control all aspects of a student's education, Rousseau also suggested the revolutionary concept that teachers transition their role from a dictator of knowledge to a facilitator of student learning (Guisepi, 2007). Although Rousseau's ideas received significant criticism, he nevertheless provided the impetus for future philosophers to expand on his groundbreaking concepts.

John Dewey pushed Rousseau's ideas further to develop his own educational philosophy that served as the predecessor of authentic learning. Dewey borrowed from the ideas of famous psychologist and child development theorist Jean Piaget, who proposed that children gain knowledge of the world in stages. Unlike previous philosophers that espoused intelligence as a fixed biological trait much like height or eye color, Piaget suggested that intelligence occurs over time and in stages resulting from a child's prolonged interaction with his/her environment. In fact, children "construct" their environments through different schemas based on their understanding of reality (McLeod, 2015). Dewey expanded upon Piaget's theories to relate constructivism to education. Specifically, the educational theory of constructivism proposed that students actively "construct" their own knowledge from personal experience rather than passively accepting information from teachers (Lewis & Williams, 1994). In fact, Dewey believed that teachers should build on students' previous real-world experiences by relating students' prior knowledge to new ideas. This technique, known as scaffolding, originated with Locke; however, Dewey expanded this notion to suggest that students learn in gradual or incremental stages rather than simultaneously acquiring diverse and isolated facts (Peterson, 2002).

Based on his theorizing about the way in which students learn, Dewey proposed that all students learn in different ways, which exposed the weaknesses of the teacher-centered school system that delivers mass-produced, "industrial" education (Prince EA, 2016; Revington, 2016; Robinson, 2010). Accordingly, Dewey rejected the homogenous notion of education that envisioned all children as identical vessels passively awaiting the input of information from an all-knowing teacher. Rather, he posited that each student possesses his or her own unique strengths, weaknesses, needs, and interests that characterize a heterogeneous rather than a homogenous approach to education. From this perspective, Dewey served as the predecessor to contemporary theories of multiple intelligences, most recently elaborated by Howard Gardner in his book *Frames of mind: The theory of multiple intelligences*. In this book, Gardner proposes that individuals perceive the world through at least seven different lenses: linguistic, mathematical, visual-spatial, kinesthetic, musical, interpersonal, and intrapersonal. He suggested that each person understands phenomenon through one or a few dominant ways, thus demonstrating individual differences in learning styles (Gardner, 2011). Sir Ken Robinson concurs with Gardner's theories, positing that the current conception of education holds a "narrow definition of intelligence" (Peritz, 2017) and, like Gardner, maintaining that students have different aptitudes (Robinson, 2010). Considering this wealth of knowledge that has existed for over a full century, it is truly amazing to think that the teacher-centered paradigm of education still persists, where teachers are trained to force-feed students information through only a few of these channels while completely disregarding the others.

Due to Dewey's unique perception of the student body, along with the importance of student experience, Dewey believed that traditional, teacher-centered approaches to education failed the student (Neil, 2005). Dewey envisioned a shift in the power of learning from the teacher to the student. In fact, he conceptualized education as a democratic process in which students constitute valuable members of the learning environment. From this perspective, learners possess freedom that provides them with the permission and ability to independently engage in their own intellectual inquiry (Kucey & Parsons, 2012). In fact, Robinson (2013) refers to this democratization of education when he acknowledges the important role of cultural and social aspects in the school system. Robinson argues that policymakers, administrators, and teachers ignore these important dimensions while focusing largely on the economic implications of education. While Dewey's educational philosophy articulated the concepts underpinning student-centered learning, authentic learning emerged out of Dewey's constructivism, focusing especially on the way in which educational experience started with the student rather than the teacher.

Authentic learning, which comprises the bulk of the next chapter, is often conceived as a branch of constructivism that emanated from the educational philosophy of John Dewey. Orey (2010) stated that constructivism provides a social context for learning that allows students to construct their own knowledge from the real world. As one of the pioneers for student-centered learning, Dewey rejected the traditional, teacher-centered methods of education and advocated for practical learning based on real-life contexts. Specifically, Dewey proposed an interrelationship between education and democracy, which conceives students as independent beings with the freedom to explore their own inquiries (Kucey & Parsons, 2012). One of the main tenets of this methodology necessitates an integration between theoretical knowledge and practical experience (Westbrook, 1993). In opposition to the notion of the student as a blank slate for teachers to fill with knowledge, Dewey envisioned each student as a vessel containing a unique set of prior information and experiences. Consequently, he believed that teachers should build upon the students' existing knowledge base by guiding rather than dictating their learning experiences. One of the ways in which Dewey suggested instructing students entailed the use of problem solving as a way of generating student inquiry and ultimately learning (Radu 2011; Westbrook, 1993), which recalls the ancient Socratic method described earlier in the chapter. This insight led to the use of problem solving and questioning as one of the pedagogical methods that comprise constructivism, a branch of student-centered learning.

Within the ideology of constructivism, each student is an individual learner who constructs his/her own knowledge by building on prior knowledge. Although constructivism, which originated from Dewey, Piaget, and other philosophers and psychologists, has resulted in the evolution of many different student-centered educational approaches, this project will focus mainly on authentic learning as a subset of constructivism. Authentic learning, as described more fully in the subsequent chapter, involves the provision of "real world" contexts in which student learning can take place. Educators who utilize this pedagogical methodology provide realistic problems or situations that contain both personal relevance and a real-life setting (Renzulli et al., 2004). Students that engage in active learning can explore these situations in order to construct personal meaning through the connection between prior knowledge and new information, hence relating authentic learning to constructivism.

An exploration of the evolving philosophies and purposes of education demonstrate that throughout history, the objectives of education have always remained congruent with the needs of society. However, despite the emergence of today's knowledge-based or creative economy, discussed extensively in Chapter 6, education systems at all levels remain mired in the past, thus failing to achieve the aims of society. This lack of alignment between education and society underlies the purpose of this book: to suggest the implementation of authentic learning strategies in African postsecondary schools. The next chapter advances Dewey's revolutionary philosophies to conduct an in-depth examination of the main theoretical framework defining this book: authentic learning.

CHAPTER THREE
AUTHENTIC LEARNING

Learning by Creating a Tangible and Useful Product

IN THE 2006 MOVIE *ACCEPTED*, PROTAGONIST BARTLEBY Gaines accuses Richard Van Horne, the dean of a rival college, of "rob[bing] these kids of their creativity and their passion" (Pink, 2006) when referring to Van Horne's own college, which follows the traditional ways of learning. Bartleby, who had created his own college, known as the South Harmon Institute of Technology (ironically with the acronym of S.H.I.T.), must defend his college against Dean Van Horne's charges that the South Harmon Institute of Technology is a fraudulent institution (Pink, 2006). Bartleby eventually wins his case, awarded the ability to keep his institution alive and provide students with an alternative method of learning, where students have the freedom to not only choose their own classes but also create their own curricula. Bartleby's words eerily echo those spoken by Prince EA, who maintained that schools have been "killing creativity [and] individuality" (Prince EA, 2016). Both sources of popular fiction consider modern dysfunctional school systems in terms of a criminal offence; Prince EA accuses schools of "intellectual abuse" and "educational malpractice" (Prince EA, 2016) while, during his trial defense, Bartleby accuses Dean Van Horne of a "real crime" (Pink, 2006). The purpose of this book, as suggested in the prologue, involves stopping this heinous crime of educational malpractice and fixing it with the student-centered learning approach of authentic learning.

While the previous chapter provided an approximate timeline of educational development around the world, the current chapter situates the student-centered approach of authentic learning within that framework. Much research controversy exists pertaining to the true origin and definition of authentic learning. Most authors generally consider authentic learning as an educational approach that provides real-life contexts for learning (Renzulli, Gentry, & Reis, 2004), thus implying the potential existence of several possible teaching methods that can be considered as authentic learning. Due to its broad nature, authentic learning can incorporate all phases of the teaching and learning process, including planning, delivery, assessment, and evaluation (Fry, Ketteridge, & Marshall, 2009; Maina, 2004; Peterson, 2002). Authentic learning resembles its predecessor, constructivism, in its attempt to help students to construct personal meaning out of their learning experiences by connecting previous knowledge with new information (Mims, 2003).

Apart from its association with constructivism and real-life learning, however, the educational literature disagrees on the scope and scale of authentic learning. Mattar (2010) takes a microcosmic perspective in classifying authentic learning as a methodology incorporated under the general category of constructivism, while Maina (2004) considers authentic learning as a principle that comprises all forms of constructivist learning, thus conceiving authentic learning on a macroscale rather than a microscale. Steve Revington, who provides the most detailed and precise definition of authentic learning, departs from these conventional perspectives to argue that authentic learning differs from constructivism in several ways, most notably by virtue of its location within the community rather than the classroom. Further researchers posit that authentic learning closely resembles other forms of active, student-centered learning, such as experiential learning (Knobloch, 2003). In order to resolve this controversy, this book will utilize the definition and conceptualization of authentic learning based on the principles of Steve Revington, an award-winning Canadian educator. First, however, we will take a look at other types of student-centered learning in order to provide a methodological context for authentic learning.

FORMS OF STUDENT-CENTERED LEARNING

Prior to discussing the principles of authentic learning, this chapter will briefly explicate other forms of active, student-centered learning with which authentic learning has been associated. While many different types of these instructional methods exist, the three most relevant to authentic learning include personalized learning, gameful or game-based learning, and experiential learning. Although other student-centered learning methods exist, and the connection between the various methods can overlap, this study identifies the three most popular forms of student-centered learning that commonly relate to authentic learning.

Personalized Learning

In the film *Accepted*, Bartleby provides his students with what one can consider personalized learning. He begins by asking his students "What do you want to learn?" (Pink, 2006). In fact, this is the very question that Mr. Luke Ddumba, my history teacher, asked me on the first day of my Senior 5 history class, one of the few examples of student-centered learning that I experienced in my entire educational history along with, of course, my master's program. In response to Mr. Ddumba, we collaboratively defined our educational objectives for that semester. In the film, the students write down everything that they want to learn, ranging from cooking to meditation, providing a cruder interpretation than the one I experienced in senior high. Although personalized learning exists differently in the real world, it nevertheless comprises a form of student-centered learning that, like other active learning methods, centers the experience around the student. However, while many student-centered methods can still treat the students as a single body or mass of learners, personalized learning emphasizes the uniqueness of each student by customizing the education process to each student's strengths, weaknesses, needs, and interests (Patrick, Kennedy, & Powell, 2013). Prince EA and Suli Breaks, the two spoken word artists introduced in the beginning of the book, advocate desperately for this type of learning to replace the outdated and dysfunctional education system, while Ken Robinson proposes a call to action in which governments and policymakers make education more personalized and customized (Strauss, 2015).

As is the case with authentic learning, personalized learning constitutes an ambiguous term, as many conceptions of this learning style exist based on any combination of personalized timing, delivery, content, access, resources, and location (Paludan, 2006). In many cases, personalized learning exploits modern technology, including computers, internet, and mobile devices, to allow students to explore their own interests and provide them with personalized learning portals to access their course information, including learning activities, correspondence, and assessments from any time and place (Garry & Phillips, 2013). To this extent, many modern educational institutions in North America and Europe have embraced this initiative alongside the traditional lecture method. As in the case of authentic learning, personalized learning incorporates assessment strategies that use formative methods through collaboration between teacher and student (Patrick et al., 2013). Teachers or instructors can combine personalized learning with traditional forms of instruction to create a style known as blended learning (Garry & Phillips, 2013; Patrick et al., 2013). In fact, some scholars have even proposed a style of learning that combines three educational platforms: in-person, online, and digital media (AIR, 2013). One variation of blended learning, termed the inverted classroom, requires students to engage in pre-class activities, such as independent reading or viewing of theoretical material, prior to attending class, where the teacher subsequently engages students in interactive activities, such as collaborative group work, debates, or full class discussions (Stickel & Liu, 2015). The inverted classroom displays features of both blended and personalized learning by combining students' personal explorations of course material through online or digital formats before attending class. Personalized learning can be used in combination with other learning methods, including authentic learning, and, the next methodology, game-based learning.

Game-Based Learning

Game-based or gameful learning resembles personalized learning to the extent that each student demonstrates control over many aspects of their learning. This instructional method derives its name from the similarities between the learning process and video games, where students resemble gamers by progressing through various levels to achieve a specific goal or objective (Fishman & Holman, 2015). From this perspective, game-based learning has also been termed "goal-based learning," another closely-associated method of active learning. Goal-based learning, an offshoot of personalized learning, allows students to identify their learning goals at the beginning of the semester and design their course accordingly (AIR, 2013), similar to the way in which Mr. Ddumba approached our senior history class. However, goal-based learning lacks the specific feeling of games and gamification, which game-based learning attempts to replicate in various ways.

In game-based learning, students will, in consultation with teachers, determine their learning goal and choose their own "path" towards that goal in much the same way as gamers choose their techniques and strategies to achieve the objective. In fact, students can often choose their own method of assessment, similar to personalized learning (Fishman & Holman, 2015). The level-by-level progression of the gamer mirrors the process of scaffolding, where students must acquire more foundational knowledge before progressing to more complex concepts (Revington, 2016), thus resembling both student-centered and authentic learning. As in the case of a game, where gamers choose special boosts or power-ups to enhance their play, students can freely choose the resources that support their learning. Like a gamer, students will encounter obstacles that impede their progress; however, students can consult their teacher or instructor for feedback or additional resources (Fishman & Holman, 2015). From this perspective, game-based learning emphasizes the process of learning as much as the actual outcome.

Finally, game-based learning can also incorporate virtual or physical rewards that provide reinforcement or gratification by providing students with a type of point-based system (Wheeler, 2016). My Canadian colleague informed me that while student teaching, one of her associate teachers used the concept of "chits," token that, in accumulation, provided students with rewards ranging from a class movie to time outside the classroom. She explained that students received chits for exceptional academic performance or good behavior, such as concentrating during silent reading or helping another student in some way. Students can receive chits individually, in groups, or across the entire class, serving as a motivator and reinforcer. Finally, teachers can incorporate game-based learning into their classrooms through learning activities such as simulations, role-play, and learning games (Contact North, 2015). In fact, similar to Bartleby Gaines, who provides his students with the opportunity to learn through gaming (Pink, 2006), teachers can use video games as instructional tools that stimulate students' problem-solving, critical thinking, and multitasking (Levasseur, 2015).

Experiential Learning

Experiential learning, similar to authentic learning, provides realistic learning experiences to students. As in the case of authentic learning, experiential learning traces its origin back to the constructivist paradigm pioneered by John Dewey. Experiential learning proposes that students learn through direct experience rather than merely acquiring abstract knowledge of theories, concepts, and processes (Lewis & Williams, 1994). In this method of student-centered learning, students directly experience aspects of the real world and subsequently reflect upon these experiences in a journal (Knobloch, 2003). One of the most common examples of experiential learning occurs in the education program, where students write about their experiences of practice teaching. As my Canadian colleague informed me, the process of writing reflective journals on incidents that happened during her teaching practicum helped her to analyze her own reaction to certain situations and make future adaptations to her teaching practice. Likewise, nursing students often write reflective journals on experiences that occur during their clinical rotations with evidence from scholarly nursing journals, thus relating theory directly to practice as per authentic learning.

Similarly, experiential learning forces students to take complete responsibility for their own learning (Moon, 2004). Experiential learning bears some similarities to other types of active learning, inquiry-based learning, which stimulates students' natural curiosity and motivates them to learn, and problem-based learning, which initiates the learning experience through the presentation of a problem that students must subsequently solve either independently or in collaborative groups (Motlhaka, 2014). Teachers facilitate the process of inquiry-based learning by continually prodding students with questions to encourage further exploration while providing hints, tips, and feedback that keep them interested in the learning process (Oblinger, 2007). The continual use of questioning used in inquiry-based learning clearly has its roots in the Socratic method discussed in the previous chapter. In fact, Knobloch (2003) argues that experiential learning meets most of the criteria of authentic learning based on inductive problem solving, active use of knowledge, and application of knowledge beyond the classroom. However, experiential learning differs from authentic learning by virtue of its location in the classroom rather than the community. Accordingly, the remainder of this chapter will focus solely on authentic learning as the main methodology with which this book is concerned.

AUTHENTIC LEARNING

Principles of Authentic Learning

Due to the research controversy surrounding the ideological location of authentic learning on the spectrum of student-centered learning, this book will use the criteria enumerated by Steve Revington (2016) due to the clear and strict limitations that they pose. Although other authors, including Oblinger (2007) and Herrington (2009), prescribe characteristics of authentic learning, Revington's principles most clearly differentiate authentic learning from other methodologies with which it is easily confused. On his website, Revington provides an explicitly detailed definition of authentic learning, including the criteria that such a model must fulfill. In concurrence with the rest of the literature, Revington (2016) describes authentic learning as "real life learning … that encourages students to create a tangible, useful product to be shared with their world" (para. 1). In fact, one of the Makerere University professors characterizes successful teaching on the basis of students' ability to "produce something that [he] can see" (C. Mugimu, personal communication, April 28, 2017), thus concurring with Revington about the necessity of a tangible product as evidence of successful teaching. Based on the worlds "real life," "tangible" and "useful," authentic learning resembles the Indigenous methods of learning discussed in Chapter 1, including the education of Canadian Aboriginal students and IAE. Echoing the literature, Revington (2016) asserts that the process and the product of authentic learning share equal importance. While other authors maintain that authentic learning resembles other types of active, student-centered learning, including game-based learning (Fishman & Holman, 2015) or experiential learning (Knobloch, 2003), Revington (2016) clearly and purposely differentiates authentic learning from these other modes by the fact that while other active learning methods occur solely in the classroom, authentic learning involves some type of community interaction that exceeds the bounds of the classroom. In addition to Revington, Ken Robinson (2013) argues that education must strive for a greater connection between schools and the world outside the schools, as currently, this link is missing.

The Elements of Authentic Learning

On his website, Revington (2016) lists twelve elements that qualify as authentic learning and distinguishes this instructional methodology from other forms of active, student-centered learning. These elements include 1) a tangible product, 2) a clearly-defined community audience, 3) design-back planning, 4) well-defined criteria, 5) role playing, 6) integrated subjects, 7) blended scheduling, 8) collaboration, 9) personalized experience, 10) portfolios, 11) master consultation, and 12) community involvement. First, a tangible product must be "original" and "shared with the world," thus emphasizing the innovative aspect of authentic learning (Revington, 2016, para. 2). The second element, the requirement of a community audience, elaborates on the criteria for the tangible product. Specifically, Revington states that the product, service, or event needs to be targeted to a specific audience and designed for that group. In order to achieve this purpose, Revington suggests that teachers solicit information from community experts, which relates to the elements of master consultation and community involvement. Third, Revington proposes the concept of design-back planning for teachers creating authentic learning opportunities. After establishing the target audience and purpose of the product, teachers need to outline aspects such as "skill sets, support information, curriculum connections, learning processes, human and material resources" (Revington, 2016, para. 5). The fourth element, well-defined criteria, must align with the planning and the audience and include quality expectations that are communicated with the students and other stakeholders. Revington departs from most scholars to maintain that "skill development resembles spirals rather than rigid steps." (para. 6). Thus, the concept of scaffolding contains circular rather than linear progression.

The fifth element, role playing involves the creative aspect of allowing students to fully immerse themselves in the role of another person, thus increasing the students' motivation and productivity. Role playing relates to collaboration, especially when students take "on a role of a position within a team" with "a specific job description" (para. 7). Integrated subject areas, the sixth authentic learning element, relate to real life because "in real life situations, most undertakings are not subject specific" (para. 8). Authentic learning integrates subject areas to teach students specific criteria, as in element four, rather than a subject. The element of integrated subjects relates to the seventh element, blended scheduling, in which the "subject timetable goes out the window" (para. 8). In blended scheduling, teachers require large blocks of time to implement and deliver authentic learning activities and experiences, thus allowing "for creativity and deeper focus to flourish" (para. 9). The element of collaboration, a team-based approach, involves the development of team skills through partnerships, small-group, and large-group activities. Through these scenarios, students can learn social interaction and cooperation, both skills that are required in the real world.

Revington's ninth element, personalized experience, incorporates some aspects of personalized learning into authentic learning. Although authentic learning opportunities involve team or group situations, teachers need to provide students with the opportunity to "explore their personal interests and creativity" (para. 13). This element not only invokes the real-world skill of creativity, thus overlapping with the tangible product element, but also acknowledges that different people approach learning with different values, backgrounds, and interests, as emphasized throughout this book. In personalized learning, "each student creates their own story" (para. 14). Part of personalized learning involves the development of student portfolios, which constitutes the tenth element of authentic learning. Portfolios involve "a collection of papers and artifacts of learning that support student research, record ideas, drafts, consultation notes, lists, diagrams, worksheets, reflection notes, articles, dimensions and even budgets" (para. 15). Portfolios relate to real life because "they are essential in the workplace just as any designer or executive would have them" (para. 15). The eleventh element, master consultation, involves "connecting to experts in the community who can provide quality input" (para. 16). These experts can provide "quality skills, expert consultations, quality resources, workmanship, and planning" (para. 16), thereby providing many different products, services, and resources to teachers and students. This element connects to authentic learning because "students are interacting directly with the real world" (para. 16). Revington maintains that without real-world interaction, the learning experience fails to quality as "authentic." Finally, the element of professional development concerns the evolution of the teacher's role from "content dispenser" to an "event coordinator, consultant, or facilitator" (para. 17). When planning authentic learning opportunities, teachers often gain new skillsets about learning new technologies, products, services, or people, thus allowing them to model new skills and processes for students.

As emphasized in the previous paragraphs, one common thread among all of Revington's elements involves their interrelationship with one another, as parts of one element depend upon or overlap with parts of another. Taken overall, these aspects emphasize the product, the audience, the planning, the teacher's role, and the student's role. The products created from the authentic learning experience include the tangible product or outcome that the students have created and shared with the community, while the creation of student portfolios represent another product of the authentic learning experience. Unlike the actual tangible product, which society can use or consume, the portfolio represents the process rather the outcome, documenting notes, diagrams, pictures, reflections, articles, and spreadsheets (Revington, 2016). Other educators have recommended the use of portfolios as a means of displaying student work, including that of education students. These portfolios demonstrate authentic learning through their connection between student work and the real world (Clementz & Pitt, 2002). In fact, my Canadian colleague informed me that as an education student preparing for the transition from graduation to employment, she was encouraged to keep a portfolio for display to potential employers, which links education to the real world. In addition to providing a tangible product as the final learning outcome, authentic learning also emphasizes the role of a real audience. Revington (2016) insists that the teacher and/or students involved in an authentic learning experience must define the target audience, understand their interest, and gear the final product towards this audience. Furthermore, the target audience must exist outside of the confines of the school in order for the learning experience to truly classify as "authentic."

Stripped down to its most basic form, authentic learning centers on the relationship between the teacher and the student, focusing solely on the teaching and learning exchange rather than the external distractions, such as curricula, syllabi, testing, unions, schedules, and policies (Robinson, 2013). The teacher's role in the authentic learning experience differs starkly from that in traditional instructor-centered learning methods. Revington (2016) encapsulates the teacher's role as that of "a guide on the side or an event manager, a facilitator not a dictator" (para. 1); likewise, Robinson posits that the role of the teacher involves "encouraging, mentoring, [and] coaching" (Strauss, 2015). This "facilitator" or "mentor" role runs through all stages of the teaching process, including planning, scheduling, delivering, and assessing. As is the case in all student-centered learning experiences, the teacher must clearly define the criteria; however, the criteria must correspond to the intended audience and be collaboratively shared or even derived in consultation with the students. Once the teacher has defined the criteria, he/she must ensure that the students can reasonably achieve these criterion through the use of scaffolding, or multi-level instruction, which involves building upon student's current knowledge in small steps as a way of bridging the gap from their current understanding to the desired objectives (Peterson, 2002). Authentic learning also eschews the traditional compartmentalization of subjects by integrating all or most subject areas within a single authentic learning experience. As Revington (2016) asserts, real-life situations, tasks, or trades involve many skills that derive from a wide range of subject areas, thus echoing the Indigenous learning discussed in Chapter 2. Although teachers using authentic learning need to state their objectives from various subject areas to meet curricular guidelines, the experiences themselves demonstrate a seamless integration of all subjects. Accordingly, the timetable and scheduling of authentic learning activities reflects the integration of subject areas. Rather than scheduling subject areas into distinct timeframes, teachers need to plan large blocks of time that allow for deeper thinking and creativity (Revington, 2016). Finally, teachers serve as facilitators by providing consultation to students throughout the learning process. As consulters, teachers connect students to community resources, which include experts, skills, and materials (Revington, 2016).

As a form of student-centered learning, authentic learning highlights the importance of student involvement in their own education. Three aspects of student-centered learning mentioned in the previous sections, role playing, collaboration, and personalized experience, all fulfill a necessary role in authentic learning. Role playing involves students imagining themselves in the jobs, trades, or positions of other people or professionals by dressing and acting as these individuals (Revington, 2016). In addition to immersing themselves in the lives of others, role playing also overlaps with collaborative learning, where students must form groups and decide upon their role within that particular group. Collaborative learning, an element found in all aspects of active learning, imitates the real world because, in their prospective careers, people work in teams and partnerships. In addition, collaborative learning allows students to develop social skills (Revington, 2016). My Canadian colleague told me about a variation of collaborative learning or mentorship that she witnessed during one of her practicums; the associate teacher allowed, at various points, students to "be the teacher." These situations provided students with empowerment and motivation to share their knowledge and experience with their colleagues. Finally, personalized experiences provide students with control over their own learning. An integral part of personalized learning, discussed in the previous section, personalized experiences cater to the needs, strengths, weaknesses, and interests of individual students. By offering students the opportunity to have input into their learning through an exploration of their interests and creative touch, teachers will increase students' ownership and hence motivation (Revington, 2016).

Application of Authentic Learning

Based on Revington's definition of authentic learning, this educational philosophy involves several different teaching and learning methods, including multi-level instruction, scaffolding, heterogeneous groups, and the incorporation of student interests, as mentioned in the example of students playing the role of teacher. In particular, the techniques of multi-level instruction and scaffolding allow students to progress seamlessly from one level of knowledge and capability to the next level (Peterson, 2002). As per the methodology of inquiry-based learning, teachers implementing authentic learning can begin the instructional process by providing students with a challenge, problem, or question that relates to the real world and involves realistic contexts (Renzulli, Gentry, & Reis, 2004). This process, elaborated upon in Chapter 6 with the provision of contests to solve real-world problems, allows students to construct personal meaning out of their learning experiences by linking previous knowledge with new information as per the instructional technique of scaffolding (Mims, 2003).

After posing the initial question or challenge, teachers can incorporate authentic learning by providing ongoing activities or projects that include several essential characteristics: a series of multistep tasks, open-ended questioning, problem solving, the examination of issues from several different viewpoints, collaborative or cooperative learning, reflective practice, the integration of skills and knowledge from various curricular areas, and the accommodation of multiple solutions or answers (Renzulli et al., 2004). In fact, as already mentioned, many undergraduate and graduate programs incorporate reflective practice as a form of assessment that links theory to practice. At the postsecondary level, these activities, depending on the subject of instruction, can incorporate problem-based learning, project learning, experiential learning, games, simulations, role-playing, debates, realistic data sets, reflection, internships or field placements, and group projects (Bell, 2010; Royal Roads University, 2014). Although authentic learning contains ideological differences from other forms of student-centered learning, these various modes of active learning can be incorporated within authentic learning experiences.

In addition, authentic learning also involves unique assessment techniques, which include both formative and summative assessment. While summative assessment tests students' knowledge at the end of a particular course unit, formative assessment involves an ongoing evaluation of student learning. Research has shown that formative assessment used in authentic learning provides both students and teachers with benefits; while this method enables teachers to adjust their teaching approaches, students have experienced improved learning outcomes (Stull, Varnum, Ducette, Schiller & Bernacki, 2011). In authentic learning, teachers can assess students at all stages of the activity, thus providing formative assessment (Oblinger, 2007). Since authentic learning usually involves a culminating activity or project (Revington, 2016), this instructional method also includes an aspect of summative assessment. The exact assessment techniques used in authentic learning also reflect realistic and meaningful experiences, objectives, and expectations (Frey, Schmitt, and Allen, 2012). In fact, Oblinger (2007) maintains that the assessments used in authentic learning activities must seamlessly integrate with the learning activities. However, the literature contains a paucity of the qualities or guidelines defining authentic assessment.

On his website, Steve Revington provides numerous examples of authentic learning projects that he facilitated. In one project, termed the Medieval Market Living Museum, students in grades five and six created an authentic medieval trade persona in order to learn about the way in which medieval markets operated. Although the project is intended mostly for the junior level of elementary school, teachers can adapt this project to the primary (grades 1-6) or middle school (grades 7-9) levels (Revington, 2016). In order to create their persona, students needed to make an appropriate costume, a tool or product reflecting their trade, and a stall in which they pretended to market their trade. This single project intersected the various areas of the curriculum, including spelling, writing, reading, math, drama, art, and technology; for each of these areas, students completed worksheets related to the project and collected them in a portfolio; these worksheets, along with other artifacts, were utilized for formative assessment. In the culmination of the project, students presented their trade persona to outside visitors from the community, who interacted with the students by asking them questions, watching them work, listening to their stories, and reading their notes (Revington, 2016). This project meets all of the criteria that Revington includes in his definition of authentic learning. Although the project involved primary-school students, teachers can apply the same mindset to teaching at the university level, as discussed in subsequent sections of this chapter.

History of Authentic Learning

Arguably, authentic learning originated thousands of years ago with Indigenous education, as detailed extensively in Chapter 2. Across the world, Indigenous societies educated their youth on the basis of their projected trades and taught children all aspects of their profession through real-life techniques such as observation, practice, and performance (Gray, 2008). Even during the craft guild periods of education that occurred during the Middle Ages, students learned via apprenticeship; however, as the population grew, and the age of enlightenment and the scientific revolution arose, society prioritized ideas and theories over practical vocation-based learning (Oblinger, 2007). The development of teacher education approaches, which began with the craft or apprenticeship model, reflects this cyclical trend of education that began with the Craft Model, moved towards the Applied Science Model, and recently began the transition towards the reflective model, which involves the construction of journals. The Craft Model envisions the student as a type of trainee or apprentice working with an expert teacher and imitating the techniques of the experienced teacher. Next, the Applied Sciences Model perceives education as a type of science that educates teachers with research-based empirical theories about education and assesses students on their ability to apply these theories in practice. Finally, the Reflective Model emphasizes the ability of the novice teacher to achieve competence by reflecting on his or her own practice (Gambhir, Broad, Evans, & Gaskell, 2008). The Craft Model reflects Indigenous learning through the emphasis on apprenticeship, while the Applied Sciences model mirrors the Industrial age, teacher-centered modality, and finally, the Reflective Model resembles authentic learning by the provision of critical thinking.

While Indigenous learning has existed for millennia, Har (2005) argues that the actual terminology defining "authentic" learning dates back as early as the sixteenth century; at this time, Descartes proposed the notion of authenticity in conjunction with morality, where people could acquire ethical principles through learning rather than through genetics or social status (Har, 2005). After the introduction of formalized schooling that catered to a manufacturing-based economy, authentic learning reentered the education system as an offshoot of John Dewey's constructivism, as discussed at the conclusion of the previous chapter. Keefe (1989) recounts that authentic learning first entered the modern school system as early as the 1970s and has been evolving ever since that period. Prior to the advent of modern information and communication technology, authentic learning took place in the form of outdoor learning and field trips. Hein (1999) discusses the value of community-based visits to locations such as museums, while Szczepanski (2006) argues that that environmental or outdoor education enhances student motivation as well as educational attainment and overall student wellness. Based on Revington's

(2016) definition of authentic learning, these activities fulfill the criteria because the learning experience takes place in the community rather than the classroom.

Authentic Learning in the Twenty-First Century

While authentic learning can exist without the incorporation of a high-tech environment, the emergence of modern information and communication technology has greatly expanded the range of possibilities within the field of authentic learning. Computers, internet, mobile devices, and their associated applications and platforms have permeated all aspects of society, thus making these technologies completely relevant to society and hence realistic (Oblinger, 2007). Students of all ages communicate and socialize largely via digital media, indicating the need for authentic learning to fully embrace these devices (Herrington & Herrington, 2007; Lombardi, 2007). Although the Internet entered the phase of full-scale implementation in the mid-1990s, educators have lagged behind in their efforts to utilize this tool in their classrooms, as they only began to incorporate web-based education in the late 2000s through the use of the Internet to deliver education and provide learning material (Slepkov, 2008). Information and communication technology entered school curricula in the late 1980s or early 1990s. Hill and Smith (1998) discuss the integration of technology into the traditional science curriculum to create the new science and technology strand in the Canadian province of Ontario. Before 1989, technology represented an elective or optional course in secondary school; however, the Ontario elementary curriculum incorporated science and technology as a separate curricular strand (Sattler, 2011). Although these curricular developments enhanced the importance of information and communication technology in education, the use of technology in delivering student-centered or authentic learning experiences occurred much later. Educators began consistently implementing modern technology, including computers, internet, and handheld devices after 2000. Herrington (2009) discusses the way in which teachers can utilize technology to deliver authentic learning experiences to students. Although instructors use technology as a medium for the delivery of education, Herrington (2009) insists that teachers can more fully utilize the capabilities of the Internet and mobile devices to conduct authentic learning experiences by teaching students about the technology itself and encouraging students to interact with these media. Strategies for more effectively incorporating technology in authentic learning will be discussed throughout the remainder of this book, including Chapter 5 through to Chapter 8.

Authentic Learning in Postsecondary Education

Although authentic learning can occur successfully at all levels of education, the scope of this study focuses solely on the incorporation of authentic learning at the postsecondary level, including universities, colleges, and technical institutes. Herrington and Herrington (2006) assert that postsecondary instructors should facilitate authentic learning by providing students with a series of complex and multifaceted tasks that occur over an entire unit, semester, or year. One specific example of authentic learning involved a research project in a finance class, which required students to study a country of their choice and apply class concepts to the economy of that particular nation. The authors found that this task increased student engagement and enhanced their capacity to understand and solve realistic problems (Hui & Koplin, 2011). Other authors propose the use of a portfolio as a form of authentic learning at all stages of education. These portfolios contain collections or artifacts of student work samples, especially as they link the educational experience to the community. Some of the contents of these portfolios include drafts, maps, diagrams, instructions, letters, pictures, transcripts, reports, evaluations, field notes, reflections, and digital media (Clementz & Pitt, 2002; Revington, 2016). These portfolios not only relate learning to the outside world but also contain physical artifacts from the real world.

In addition, authentic learning at the postsecondary level exploits modern technology. Technology-based authentic learning experiences incorporate electronic resources and interactive digital media that mimics realistic environments, such as simulation-type experiences (Royal Roads University, 2014). Some of these simulations relate to classroom-based learning while others link the student to the professional environment. In the former case, Campbell (2013) studied the impact of a database with multi-language video explanations on students in a first-year mathematics class, finding that students with access to the videos experienced improved examination results. Furthermore, Herrington and Herrington (2006) discuss simulated or web-based learning that mimics the job setting. As a specific example of this phenomenon, Miron, O'Sullivan, and McLoughlin (2000) present an online learning environment for first-year undergraduate computer science students. This approach provides a realistic setting that allows students to gain practical knowledge and experience of their desired career. Errington (2011) proposed the implementation of scenario-based classroom learning, which replaces or supplements professional placement programs. This learning method, which allows a transition that bridges classroom theory with work experience, is most effectively implemented with technology that simulates the job environment.

In addition to digital simulations, some of the technology that fosters authentic learning experiences in postsecondary education include collaborative wikis, graphing calculators, social media, blogging, asynchronous discussion forums, and mobile computing (Atkinson, 2011). For example, students can use digital and social media to provide students with greater opportunities for solving complex problems (Herrington & Herrington, 2006). Faulkner and Faulkner (2012) examine the implementation of authentic learning in a software engineering course, where students use industry case studies, software tools, and social media to facilitate their learning. These authors found that this experience provided students with greater motivation and engagement. The use of technology-mediated authentic learning in the postsecondary environment provides several benefits to students, including increased access to education, immediate feedback, time-relevant information, increased accountability, and enhanced collaboration (Kanuka, 2008). These benefits undergo further discussion in Chapter 7, which discusses the advantages of authentic learning to several stakeholders, including students, teachers, and employers in the labor market.

Relevance of Authentic Learning to Labour Market

In the film *Accepted*, Bartleby provides his students with "jobs," thus connecting the academic realm with the labor market. Although this film serves as a comedic look at the education system, the humor veils serious ills in the inability in education to fulfill the needs of the labor market. As discussed in Chapter 5, the global labor market has steadily evolved towards increasingly specialized forms of labor (Dobbin, 2009). The transition from an industrial to a knowledge or service economy requires different educational models. During the industrial revolution, as previously documented by the spoken word artists introduced at the outset of the book, the educational system underwent transformation to reflect the structured, scheduled, and regimented atmosphere of the factory (Sawyer, 2008). However, this structure, which remains in place, fails to align with the contemporary creative economy. One Ugandan professor remarked that, "the labor market requires somebody who is more practical, more hands-on, but the school system has not bothered to produce such a student because of the challenges within the school system" (N. Itaaga, personal communication, April 20, 2017). Although these challenges will undergo further examination in the later chapters of the book, it is sufficient to highlight the gross mismatch between the current industrial educational paradigm and the required skills in today's creative economy.

While the shift towards the creative economy has already occurred in developed countries, the economies in African nations have begun to adopt a service-oriented workforce that requires unique skills, including communication, collaboration, research, synthesis, and analysis (Barron & Darling-Hammond, 2008). In fact, one of the definitions of authentic learning involves its ability to "mimic the work of professionals in the discipline" (Rule, 2006, p. 2). Today's labor markets mainly attract graduates from postsecondary institutions, thus attesting to the critical role that universities and colleges fulfill in replenishing the workforce and stimulating the economy and its individual sectors (Sattler, 2011). In all countries, employers require graduating students to learn practical skills that they can transfer immediately to their new profession (Oblinger, 2007). Despite this requirement, many postsecondary programs and courses still use teacher-centered methods of instruction, which primarily involve lecturing and rote learning (Parker, Maor, & Herrington, 2013). Herrington and Herrington (2006) maintain that higher learning instructors implement instructivist, or teacher-centered, approaches in order to adhere to the tradition of formal university teaching and cater to large classes in lecture halls while upholding the elitist image associated with university education (European Commission, 2014). However, this style of teaching results in graduates that lack adequate preparation for the workforce, as they fail to understand the way in which the theoretical knowledge and skills that they acquired in university translate into professional practice (Herrington & Herrington, 2006; Jones, Casper, Dermoudy, Osborn, & Yates, 2010).

Despite the traditional approach to university lecturing, many postsecondary institutions and programs, especially in developed countries, have increasingly incorporated a practical component, which may include a work placement, practicum, internship, apprenticeship, or cooperative education experience (Oblinger, 2007). Sattler (2011) discusses the implementation of work-based learning in Ontario's postsecondary sector. The goal of this initiative sought to strengthen connections among students, institutions, employers, and community organizations, thus providing the student with practical work experience. For instance, Resnick (1987) suggested the idea of bridging apprenticeships, which connect theoretical learning in the classroom to the application of practical knowledge in the workplace. Despite the fact that this idea occurred more than thirty years ago, my Canadian colleague informed me that during her education degree there was virtually no connection between her classroom sessions and her practicums. Although her classroom professors, formerly classroom teachers themselves, provided some activity ideas and assigned the students to create lesson plans and unit plans for their assessments in the respective courses, there was no mandate to implement these directly into the practicums.

Mariappan, Monemi, and Fan (2005) investigate the concept of service learning, a community-based application of constructivism that relates classroom material to community issues. Herrington, Reeves, Oliver, and Woo (2004) suggest that realistic experiences occur not as isolated tasks but as entire courses, either in traditional face-to-face classroom settings or virtual online classrooms. However, individual institutions, programs, or classes may entirely omit practical segments. Moreover, even in the case that such experiential aspects accompany the theoretical components, the links between theory and practice may remain ambiguous due to the program requirements or the instructional methods. Finally, many students may view practical components such as apprenticeships and practicums as tedious and repressive, causing them to harbor a dislike for the course and their intended profession (Herrington et al., 2004). As my Canadian colleague recounts in her vignette, she grew to dread her practicums due to the political and bureaucratic issues that clearly interfered with student learning as well as her own progress into the profession. These cases occur more frequently during a disconnection between theory and practice. As discussed extensively in Chapter 8, all stakeholders involved in postsecondary education, including governments, curriculum or program designers, teachers, and field supervisors, need to collaborate to implement policies that provide a wholesale shift from teacher-centered to student-centered learning.

Over the last few years, collaborations between postsecondary institutions and industry partners have shown promise in their efforts to provide students with practical work experiences that relate directly to their education. One example of an integrated industrial experience that blends theory and practice involves Carleton University's Bachelor of Computer Science Internship. This program, in partnership with Shopify, allows students to work on building software as a paid employee of Shopify, one of the world's leading e-commerce platforms, for half of the course's credits (Carleton University, 2016). This program encompasses the student's entire four years, with half of the credits coming from classroom learning and the other half from the internship (Carleton University, 2016). The Shopify model doubles the regular amount of co-op experience while providing students with potential entrepreneurial experience within an organizational context (Shopify, 2016). Other initiatives resembling Shopify have begun to emerge, including the partnership between The University of the Fraser Valley and Chinook Helicopters Limited, which plans to develop a helicopter training program within the UFV Aviation Diploma Program in order to provide students with practical, hands-on experience of flying while providing the industry with adequately trained pilots (Today Media, 2016).

In SSA regions, apprenticeships are rare, especially considering the limited resources that these countries possess. Professional programs, most notably education, do incorporate professional placements; however, problems and limitations exist with these placements. There exist limited opportunities for internships due to a lack of building space. As a result, some students are left without a placement, while others receive an undesirable placement or an internship that represents a mismatch between the student's skills and desired profession and the nature of their actual placement (N. Itaaga, personal communication, April 20, 2017). In addition, Dr. Itaaga elaborates that social attitudes and expectations in SSA envision universities as elite, academic institutions that reign superior to vocational institutes. Due to the negative attitude towards vocational schooling, the administration of many universities, including Makerere, tend to diminish the importance of hands-on experience and thus reduce the number of opportunities provided to students. As a result of these limitations, students finishing their school practice still have a skills gap that prevents them from being fully ready to begin teaching in their own classrooms (M. B. Mulumba, personal communication, April 20, 2017).

In addition to practical or integrated work experiences, universities can also connect students to professional resources through initiatives such as learning hubs and skills labs. Weingarten (2017) discusses the creation of an independent organization known as the future skills lab, which facilitates the development and measurement of the soft or transferable skills discussed extensively in this book, including adaptability, resilience, problem-solving, and information synthesis. Specifically, this lab seeks to identify the important skills that workers will require in the future, ways of assessing these skills, and strategies for teaching and learning these skills (Weingarten, 2017). In addition, this lab may coordinate pilot training programs with financing from governments and corporations (Academica Group, 2017). Another suggestion involves a type of "hub" or entrepreneurial center that offers a variety of resources for students wishing to start their own business. This hub may be in the form of a laboratory, room, website, or annual fair (Algonquin College, 2016; University Hub, 2016). In fact, a few Canadian universities and colleges have already implemented a similar concept. This centre can include links to events, education, and programs, scholarships, and community resources (Algonquin College, 2016).

Despite the existence of these promising initiatives, universities in developed countries still lack a coordinated and sustained effort amongst all stakeholders in providing students with authentic learning opportunities that link them to practical job experiences. The situation of authentic learning in Africa, discussed in further detail throughout the following two chapters, requires even greater strides. Accordingly, the next chapter, Chapter 4, will discuss the development and current context of education in SSA while Chapter 5 sets the stage for the implementation of authentic learning in these countries.

CHAPTER FOUR
EDUCATION IN AFRICA

All Things Have Changed but School

MY VERY FIRST SCHOOL EXPERIENCE OF SITTING IN AN overcrowded first grade classroom with a switch-bearing teacher enforcing the repetition of strange letters from a chalkboard provides a perfect illustration of how education systems in SSA remain stagnated in their old ways. Since colonial times, African education has transitioned from Indigenous education, as discussed in the first chapter, to the formalized, teacher-centered western system of education that even I experienced as a child. As previously explained, Indigenous African education taught children vocational activities that they learned with the guidance of elders, parents, and grandparents (Majoni & Chinyanganya, 2014). Rather than learning these activities in distinct and isolated parts separated from the whole, children experienced holistic education by learning about all aspects of a trade or career as well as basic community functioning (Adeyemi & Adeyinka, 2002). However, the roots of Indigenous knowledge were replaced with formalized western education that alienated children from their cultural, linguistic, and religious traditions. In addition, this education system at all levels experiences deficiencies that contribute to the overall poverty of the region by creating a disconnect between education and the workforce, thus creating skills gaps.

A BRIEF HISTORY OF EDUCATION IN AFRICA

Although Chapter 1 provided a general summary of educational history throughout the world, this section focuses more specifically on the way in which education developed in Africa and especially SSA. Indigenous African education, discussed extensively in Chapter 1, ended with the takeover of European colonizers. The colonial governments and Christian missionaries from Europe conquered African countries in the fifteenth century. As part of the wholesale changes, they implemented a regimented school system that isolated students from their beliefs and values, replacing their ways of knowing, religion, and language with European culture. The new school systems replaced traditional African education with "literary and academic work" (Adeyemi & Adeyinka, 2002,

p. 224), which the western world considered superior to traditional African ways of knowing, as discussed in Chapter 1. Focusing specifically on the East African countries of Kenya, Uganda, Tanganyika, and Zanzibar, Ssekamwa and Lugumba (2002) discuss the various approaches to instill formal education that unfolded in different SSA nations. Although the colonizers justified their takeover of African education and society with the objective of "civilizing" the Africans, their ultimate goal involved slavery through the replication of hierarchical structures, the eradication of traditional African culture replaced by western values, and the training of African students to serve diminutive roles in colonial governments as subordinate clerks (Mosweunyane, 2013). In order to achieve their ultimate goal of colonizing Africans, European-based schools replaced the "lived experiences" of Africans, resulting in them "suffering a disconnection from [their] culture" (C. Ssempala, personal communication, April 25, 2017).

In order to achieve the goal of creating a country of slaves, similar to what Prince EA refers to as "a society of robots" (Prince EA, 2016), early SSA postsecondary education systems followed the European model of teacher-centered approaches to learning. Prior to colonial takeover, however, African postsecondary education systems actually originated from Ancient Egyptian influences that emanated from around 2000 BC. Specifically, modern African universities still retain the traditional concept of per-anhk, which comprised part of an Egyptian temple and functioned as a scriptorium, training site, and research institute while delivering higher education to religious personnel and secular academics. Over time, African universities evolved to include these aims and functions despite the predominance of western influence. In addition, early higher education systems in Africa began as part of Ethiopian Orthodox Churches that instructed students from a wide range of levels and a variety of topics, including basic literacy and numeracy as well as religious education (Lulat, 2005). These examples showed the inclusion of the Islam religion, the spiritual orientation of many native Africans, prior to the forced infusion of Christian principles.

In the nineteenth century, Christian missionaries from Europe altered the religious inclination of education in addition to "modernizing" the schools according to their perspectives of civilization. African universities, ministries, and students came to perceive the new system as one to aspire towards in order to meet new social standards. This new worldview resulted in the eradication of African linguistic, religious, and cultural traditions (Lulat, 2005). Although some countries, such as Ethiopia, evaded colonial invasion from the British and French rulers, they nevertheless established schools and universities that promoted western principles (Yamada, 2007), thus showing the extent to which western values permeated African societies and their education systems. The overall purpose of these westernized institutions and systems aimed to train an elite ruling class based on the European system of a hierarchical society (Mamdani, 1976).

In reality, however, colonial education systems sought to train African clerks and administrators that supported the ruling white governments (Global Black History, 2016), thus perpetuating the inequality among African socioeconomic classes as well as between the colonist rulers and the native Africans. This hierarchical class system, which elevated the "African Educated Elite" over the rest of the African citizens (New African, 2017), differed enormously from the more equitable, community-oriented society that defined African society. According to Vavrus et al. (2011), African countries traditionally prioritized the needs and interests of the community as a collective entity over those of the individual, thus contrasting with the western focus on individual competition and class structures. Similarly, traditional African education focused on practical, community-based knowledge that prepared students for their integration into family and community life rather than solely the competition-driven workforce (Tedla, 1996). These communal values, reflected in Indigenous African education, were eradicated upon the indoctrination of European values (Mosweunyane, 2013). From this perspective, the western education systems implemented in Africa conflicted significantly with the values and beliefs that defined SSA prior to colonial intervention. Even today, with reform underway for African education, much of the international aid comes from European countries (Lulat, 2005), thus reinforcing western control over African schools.

Although most SSA countries have achieved their independence, they still replicate colonial models in designing their schools and delivering education (Global Black History, 2016). The European influence over African education has changed the values and principles guiding the relationship between the university and the community, creating a lack of social responsibility within African communities and a disconnect between the education delivered at the university level and the needs of the labour market. In fact, many of the students receive education in westernized values, which essentially isolates them from their culture and impedes their learning by instructing them about unfamiliar activities, experiences, and modes of thinking (Matsika, 2000), recalling the experiences of one of the research participants recounted earlier in this book. Specifically, while African universities reproduce elitist values, the labour market requires practical, hands-on skills (Yamada, 2007). This issue, which authentic learning models of teaching can address, will undergo a thorough analysis in Chapter 5.

CURRENT STATE OF EDUCATION IN SSA

Since the implementation of European-based school systems, African education has suffered with resource shortages, infrastructural challenges, and outdated teaching methods, the latter of which will constitute the main focus of the book. Although recent years have witnessed some attempts to improve the education systems in African nations, the bulk of these initiatives and resources have focused on primary and secondary education rather than higher learning. For instance, the Education for All (EFA) global movement has substantially increased enrollment in primary schools, with approximately ninety percent of children attending primary school; however, these numbers drop to thirty-five percent in secondary school and five percent in tertiary or postsecondary education (Bloom, Canning, & Chan, 2006; Vavrus et al., 2011). Not only do these figures still remain significantly behind the numbers in more developed countries but also deceptively skew the reality of African education in a positive direction. Specifically, nearly thirty million students in African countries fail to achieve the minimum required education levels due to inadequate literacy and numeracy foundations, repetition of one or more grades, and the decision to discontinue their education for various reasons (United Nations, 2011; Watkins, 2013; World Bank, 2011). Some of the reasons for poor educational attainment in SSA involve widespread health concerns, AIDS, poverty, hunger, and political conflict (UNESCO, 2012; United Nations University, 2008).

In recent decades, the governments of SSA nations have increased their emphasis on education, with increasing budgets, programs, policies, and laws that promote the importance of education and the equality of education among all sectors of society. Among all levels of education, these initiatives have focused most strongly on primary education, increasing the enrollment rate from fifty-seven percent to seventy percent over a five-year span. In addition, gender equality constitutes another area of emphasis. Historically, fewer females than males have been attending schools and demonstrating adequate levels of literacy and numeracy (United Nations University, 2008); this reality mirrors my personal story in which many young girls were prevented from pursuing their education due to barriers such as the need to help out at home, the beginning of menstruation, early pregnancy/marriage, or other issues exclusive to girls. Ironically, the inability of the girls to cross the Kyetinda River due to the conventions of female modesty symbolizes the obstacles that many girls and young women faced in pursuing their education.

Despite the increased expenditures and focus on education, students in African countries, including SSA nations, are still failing to acquire the basic literacy and numeracy skills specified in the curriculum (DFID, 2012; Ruto & Rajani, 2014). A relatively high proportion of students in all African countries have repeated at least one grade; for example, nearly twenty percent, of students in Rwanda's primary and secondary schools have repeated grades in recent years (World Bank, 2011). As previously mentioned, even with educational access, this crucial lack of foundational student learning can indicate several deficiencies, including teacher performance, curricular design, and teaching methodology. While higher enrollment rates contain the positive benefit of having greater numbers of children in the education system, this increasing trend also contains disadvantages. Due to higher enrollment rates, teacher-student ratios have been as high as 1:50 or even 1:100 in some cases; these large classes and high ratios occur at all three levels of education: primary, secondary, and tertiary (Jaffer, Ng'ambi, & Czerniewicz, 2007; United Nations University, 2008; Zwiers, 2007). While the state of teacher training and the curriculum will be discussed in the last chapter of this book, an annual report by Ruto and Rajani (2014) emphasize the potential ineffectiveness of current pedagogical approaches. In addition, the deficiencies in student outcomes result from a tradeoff between ensuring universal access and providing quality education (DFID, 2012). However, this problem can be resolved through the incorporation of authentic and personalized learning approaches, which address the learning needs of a greater range of students while still providing quality education.

Regardless of the reason or combination of reasons, these harsh figures demonstrate that African students graduating from the education system lack the ability to participate effectively in the workforce. Some studies have claimed that the poor quality of education in SSA negatively affects the workforce, which, despite some degree of positive economic growth in SSA countries, still lacks the level of skilled personnel required for many professions (British Council, 2014). According to a special report by the United Nations (2013), more than 400 million young people will enter the labor market in the next twenty years. This forecasted prediction, along with the inadequacies in African education systems, points to the necessity for immediate changes in better preparing students for the workforce. The next section of the chapter, which focuses explicitly on postsecondary education, speaks more in depth about the lack of fit between the skills and interests of graduates and the workforce demands.

POSTSECONDARY EDUCATION IN SSA

Postsecondary education in SSA suffers from numerous deficits that harm individual students, employers, and the economy. African postsecondary institutions have among the lowest enrollment rates per capita in the world (Bloom et al., 2006). While enrollment rates have doubled between 2000 and 2010, the paucity of funding directed towards higher learning has led to a decrease in the number of resources available for each postsecondary student (British Council, 2014). The paucity of financial and material resources at African universities have resulted in high student-to-teacher ratios; overcrowded lecture halls; poor instructor quality; outdated communication and information technology; reduced laboratory and library facilities; and insufficient learning environments that result from infrastructural deficits such as proper lighting and electricity (Bunoti, 2010; Jaffer, et al., 2007; United Nations University, 2008; Zwiers, 2007). In particular, Bunoti (2010) found that Ugandan students experienced low quality lectures, unprofessional teacher behavior, poor instructor preparation, and the sole use of lecturing and handouts to disseminate information. These conditions, along with curricular deficiencies and undereducated instructors, further complicate students' ability to acquire the necessary information. In fact, a UWEZO Report (2013) found that the SSA curriculum at the postsecondary level lacks sufficient depth in its material to adequately prepare students for the labour market. Many postgraduate programs merely extended the subject areas taught at the undergraduate level rather than offering specialized training that prepares students for their chosen professions (Teferra & Grejin, 2010). The low quality of education throughout most of Africa has resulted in many problems within and outside of universities, including student protests, university employee strikes, and poor policy responses by governments and ministries of education (New African, 2017).

Despite the growing economic opportunities in technical and skill-based fields, the primary, secondary, and postsecondary education systems in SSA have yet to change their approaches to learning. In 2014, the President of Uganda, Yoweri Museveni entered the conversation on this topic. He dismissed the humanities fields as useless and encouraged universities to emphasize the natural sciences. In response, the University World News maintained that:

> Scientists have questioned the idea of the government supporting science at postsecondary education level when at lower levels of education science teaching is inadequate. Most schools teach science at the theoretical level but they lack learning facilities like laboratories and consumables to make it practical. (Nakkazi, 2014)

Nakkazi's reply, while highlighting the paucity of resources plaguing African postsecondary schools, also underscores the way in which education fails to meet the needs of the current workforce. Rather than dismissing the importance of the humanities field, SSA governments and policymakers need to acknowledge the humanities as a legitimate area of study, especially given the recent focus on the creative economy, as detailed in Chapter 6.

The largest social effect of an inadequate education system involves the gap between the quality of education offered at the university level and the skills required in the labour market. Corporations and employers have even stated that graduating students in SSA lack the basic skills necessary in the workforce (Materu, 2007; United Nations, 2011), leading to skills gaps in the labour market. One startling example involves the fact that while most SSA economies are largely based on agriculture, there are more graduates in every other field than in agriculture (Global Black History, 2016). Part of this problem results from the fact that many students move out of the region to pursue higher education in more suitable areas, leading to "brain drain" and depriving the local or national economy of skilled workers (British Council, 2014, p. 3). As a result, companies and industries experience a deficit of skilled workers, leading to limited productivity and profit (British Council, 2014). The low quality of higher education in SSA nations exerts detrimental effects on all parts of the workforce, most notably that of the healthcare sector. For instance, SSA countries experience twenty-four percent of the world's diseases and only comprise four percent of the world's workforce, thus illustrating significant gaps in healthcare education, which faces many financial, infrastructural, and personnel challenges (Bingawaho et al., 2013). However, healthcare and agriculture are just two examples of industries in SSA countries where immense skills gaps exist.

As shown in the personal stories of Chapter 1, there are serious individual consequences of an ineffective education system that exists in isolation from the labour market. Both my Canadian colleague and myself lacked the ability to immediately find jobs for which we were educationally qualified due to gaps between the education we received and societal needs. As a result, we took on jobs for which we were either overqualified or underqualified; my Canadian colleague languished in a food service job for more than a year before realizing that she needed more education due to systematic inefficiencies, while I entered the teaching field without any previous experience before taking on the role of an auditor without even the basics of accounting. While the personal effects of poor academic preparation include limited access to job or business opportunities, the economic consequences include low purchasing power, an unskilled workforce, and an increased crime rate (United Nations, 2011). In addition, the poor reputation of postsecondary institutions in Africa lead students to pursue higher education in other regions or other nations, depriving local economies of skilled workers, a phenomenon known as the "brain drain" (British Council, 2014). The end result of these phenomena includes the fact that at least half of the graduates produced by East African universities lacks competence for the workforce (Nganga, 2014). The Inter-University Council for East African (IUCEA) found that in five East African countries, including Uganda, Kenya,

Tanzania, Burundi, and Rwanda, approximately sixty-three percent of university graduates lack adequate job market skills (IUCEA Report, 2014).

My personal work experience mirrors the academic and scholarly reports highlighting the dire situation of African postsecondary education and its inability to adequately prepare students for the labour market. As the former Senior Program Coordinator in Rwanda, I was tasked with the responsibility of coordinating capacity building initiatives to boost the struggling Rwandan economy. My team conducted a Skills Audit (2009) and examined the country's human resources. As a result, the team discovered significant gaps in professional skillsets. In a country of twelve million people, Rwanda boasted only 171 specialist doctors, 520 general practitioners, and 180 engineers. In fact, this country only had a single neurologist at the time of the audit. My research team discovered the existence of pressure in the form of mismatched placements. Specifically, skilled professionals were often working outside of their area of training: engineers worked as administrators and doctors worked as government supervisors. As an auditor working for the RRA, I lacked even the basics in accounting, which I needed to learn on the job.

The audit also revealed large numbers of poorly trained graduates. When doctors furthered their education in South Africa, they required two more years of training before they could enroll to pursue a post-graduate degree in any of their respective chosen specialties. Consequently, electrical engineers lacked the ability make even small changes to their home electrical systems. Not unlike the scientific and medical professions, many teachers enter the school system with inadequate training, no training, or training in a completely different profession. In the process of completing my doctoral dissertation, I interviewed several professors at Makerere University, all of whom indicated that they had been hired to teach at Makerere despite their lack of training. One professor stated that: "I first entered university through a part-time position. I did not even get an invitation to teach; I came to teach postgraduate students one afternoon and that is how it started" (P. Ssenkusu, personal communication, April 20, 2017). Although other participants had acquired their doctorates, the basic requirement for teaching at the university level, some of them had their Ph.D. in other fields, such as philosophy or sciences, rather than education, while some of them taught without their doctorate for several years.

The process of interviewing Makerere professors also revealed that many university instructors treated teaching as a type of consolation prize when they lacked access to their chosen profession. A third professor admitted that he entered the teaching profession as his second choice to journalism, thus making education a type of consolation prize. He admitted that "If I did not become a journalist, then I should become a teacher" (M. B Mulumba, personal communication, April 20, 2017). Similarly, yet another participant attested to his initial lack of interest in teaching:

> At first, I was not interested in teaching. I did a B.A. in another part of the university. When I looked for a job, there were no positions, but somehow, I found a position in the Ministry of Labor. I worked there, but, as you know, the money is not there. One day, they advertised for untrained teachers because the schools had run short of teachers. After I went to the ministry to apply, I got a letter, and they posted me to Old Kampala Secondary School. (S. W. Wafula, personal communication, April 20, 2017)

Interestingly, the path that Dr. Wafula took to education bears a striking resemblance to my own path to education. With an undergraduate degree in economics, there were no jobs available for me, which eventually led to a position in the government after a few temporary jobs of private teaching. Although teaching had not necessarily been my first choice, I ended up in the education field due to the lack of qualified teachers in the system, a lack which speaks to the poor quality of education in SSA.

It is not only my experience of interviewing university professors that attests to the lack of fit between skills or passion and labor market needs. While working in the government, I acutely experienced the skills gap firsthand. Graduates of the school system were poorly equipped to implement strategies developed by international consultants and funded by international communities. The recommendations of many reports, in every sector, remained stalled on paper because Rwanda's own people lacked the administrative, organizational, and problem-solving capabilities to implement change. In tracing the roots of these human capital challenges, it is difficult to overlook the role of the school system. Unfortunately, SSA's economic failings reflected back in my own failed school experience as described in the book's first chapter. Despite the use of the word "failed," I was one of the few students who graduated; I graduated with a full scholarship, placing among the top 200 students in the country.

While I may have passed my exams, I graduated with a significant skills gap in which I lacked adequate preparation for work in the twenty-first century's creative and global economies, further discussed in Chapter 6. As my personal story reveals, I worked as an auditor in the RRA despite my lack of accounting education. In addition, like the university instructors that I interviewed in my study, I lacked the preparation to become a teacher and only accepted the job offer from a ministry official because of my desperation for employment. The lack of adequate teacher training and orientation, mentioned by my research participants, represents a significant area of concern that limits the ability of teachers to utilize effective teaching methods in instructing their students. Due to their lack of experience, along with the other factors discussed throughout this book, many teachers rely on the teacher-centered method of education that trains students to memorize, copy words from the chalkboard and fear wrong answers. Students lack the opportunity to wonder about the world around them. They do not learn to brainstorm new solutions or connect the stories of Napoleon with the stories of their own country. Creativity, innovation, critical thinking, problem solving, and social group interactions: these are the essential skills for growth in any economy. As my own story shows, these crucial learning objectives are missing in the curriculum and classrooms of SSA education systems.

Due to the plethora of problems hindering the quality of postsecondary education in SSA regions, certain educational reforms have directly targeted improvements to postsecondary education. Most governments recognize the prominent role of education in not only supplying the workforce but also improving the moral, intellectual, ideological, and cultural aspects of society (Uganda's Government White Paper on Education for Sustainable Development, 1992). Muwagga (2006) reports that governments of SSA countries have encouraged students to enter this level of education at an earlier period with the aim of reducing social inequality and creating additional opportunity for disadvantaged groups. However, as mentioned, the increased enrollment in postsecondary education has enhanced problems pertaining to resource limitations, infrastructural challenges, and teaching quality. Statistics document that one in every twenty students has access to a computer and one in nine students has access to a textbook (NCHE Report, 2014). Some proposed changes for enhancing higher education in Africa include an increase in publicly funded universities, the implementation of a student loan scheme, the development of partnerships that enhance networking, and the involvement of the private sector, such as oil industries, in tertiary education (Ssentamu, 2013). In their investigation of Uganda's Makerere University, Mugimu, Nakabugo, & Katunguka-Rwakishaya (2013) suggested the need to develop sustainable local capacity for research and teaching. These avenues represent additional funding sources that allow African universities to manage the rapidly growing enrollment rates while simultaneously increasing the quality of education. However, as the subsequent chapters will show, many challenges remain to SSA postsecondary education, including the retaining of outdated teacher-centered methods of education.

LEARNING METHODOLOGIES IN SSA

In contrast to developed and developing countries, who have transitioned or at least begun to transition towards student-centered education, African nations still lag behind in their ability to adopt student-centered methods such as authentic learning. The education systems in most African countries still implement the traditional teacher-centered pedagogy, where instructors select the material and deliver instruction through methods such as direct lecturing, memorization, rote learning, factual information, and summative assessments with paper-and-pencil tests (Vavrus, et al., 2011). My interviews with professors at Makerere University revealed that even at the postsecondary level, instructors still rely on the teacher-centered model as their go-to method of teaching. One professor stated that:

> many of our colleagues employ the traditional approaches to teaching, and the major method is the lecture method…[where] a professor, a doctor, or a lecturer stands in front of a class and talks about his subject matter to the students and then leaves the classroom. Sometimes, the students are not even given an opportunity to say something during the lecture. (M. B. Mulumba, personal communication, April 20, 2017)

As mentioned above, the persistence of the teacher-centered lecture method in SSA nations contributes largely to the inability of students to grasp the fundamental skills not only required at their level of education but also needed for the labor market. As the same instructor revealed, "There is a mismatch between the way that we train our students and the changing trends out there" (M. B. Mulumba, personal communication, April 20, 2017). As upcoming chapters will argue, the use of authentic learning methods is highly recommended for addressing the workforce skills gap and providing postsecondary students in SSA with the appropriate skills and abilities that accord to such "changing trends" mentioned in the interview.

This teacher-centered educational methodology operates under the assumption that all students have similar or equal strengths, interests, learning styles, and abilities. As mentioned, this system was originally inherited from the colonial period, where missionaries indoctrinated African students with European culture, language, and religion. Colonizers chose the teacher-centered method because it facilitated teachers' abilities to force instruction on students (Vavrus et al., 2011). Several authors cite the ineffectiveness of the current teacher-centered mode of instruction that persists in African universities (Barron & Darling-Hammond, 2008; Oblinger, 2007). For example, a study by Zwiers (2007) demonstrated that fact-based teaching failed to enable students to remember factual information after their education, especially since this type of instruction lacks relevance in the real world. King (2011) argues that the teacher-centered method of education alienates students from their teachers or instructors by virtue of the fact that students perceive teachers as distant authority figures that merely disseminate knowledge rather than facilitate learning. Although Africa has experienced many social, cultural, economic, and political changes since the inception of these early education systems, the teacher-centered methods still persist in most of these countries. As a result of their outmoded pedagogical methods, African nations produce some of the lowest educational measures and achievements on a global basis. Most aspects of African education systems still lag far behind those of developed and even developing countries, including early childhood, primary, secondary, and tertiary education as well as educational equality in categories such as gender, socioeconomic status, and regional location (EFA, 2014).

While some postsecondary school instructors acknowledge the inadequacies of their teacher-centered learning approaches, they attest to the barriers that keep them firmly entrenched in the use of such outdated pedagogies. In fact, interviews with Makerere professors provided several justifications for their continued use of the lecture method. These instructors pointed to many of the same reasons illustrated in the scholarly research, including the lack of resources, poor infrastructure, lack of appropriate training, time limitations, and outdated educational philosophies. Many professors cited inadequate resources and infrastructure as a major barrier to authentic learning. Most teachers highlighted the large class sizes, mentioning that classes can consist of up to 1000 students, which represents a highly unmanageable student load, restricting teachers to the use of the lecture method. One professor , "We are using the lecture method, basically because we lack the necessary infrastructure" (N. Itaaga, personal communication, April 20, 2017). However, another instructor disagreed that resource limitations represented a problem:

> I disagree that it is a question of resources. I can have two or three computers, projectors, white boards, and overhead projectors, but having those in place does not guarantee that I will use them to facilitate learning if I do not have the knowhow and competence to do so. (C. Mugimu, personal communication, April 28, 2017)

Basically, this response implies two things: first, that knowledge and training constitute the starting point of improving teaching methods, and secondly, that despite resource limitations, professors can still implement authentic learning methods with the right knowhow. In fact, the next chapter will highlight some of the efforts that SSA instructors facing resource limitations have made in order to attempt authentic learning methodologies at the postsecondary level.

As shown in the previous conversation snippet, another major concern among the professors highlighted the lack of knowledge and training. One professor attests to the fact that "in Makerere, there is hardly any staff development" (C. Mugimu, personal communication, April 28, 2017). In conjunction with the lack of teacher training and orientation, discussed extensively in the last chapter of the book, another issue concerns the mindset of teachers, many of whom, despite their knowledge of authentic learning approaches, experience a strong resistance or apathy towards changing their methods, especially given the numerous challenges that exist. One professor admits:

> another issue is motivation from the perspective of both staff and students … some staff may think that because they have a first-class degree, they are automatically a good teacher. This is not necessarily true; grades don't translate into passion. Some people here are not here because they want to be; it is because they have been appointed. (P. Ssenkusu, personal communication, April 20, 2017)

The fact that many teachers lack the passion for teaching corresponds to the prominent skills gap in most SSA countries, where many graduates lack the ability to find jobs in their industry and begin teaching because it presents the only viable means of employment. Thus, the lack of passion amongst teachers represents a major concern in retaining old methods of teaching.

Although a few professors highlighted their attempts to use modern, student-centered methods of learning, these attempts, while among the vast minority, encountered significant resistance from the factors described above, including resource limitations, infrastructural challenges, and prior learning philosophies. One professor states that when he introduced a type of student-centered learning that revolved around introducing a problem or challenge, "students initially found it very challenging to identify an instructional problem. It could take them weeks because they have to think very deeply and many of them have difficulties with writing and reading" (C. Mugimu, personal communication, April 28, 2017). Since most students in SSA have never been exposed to student-centered learning methods throughout the duration of their primary and secondary education, they feel confused and frustrated when rare instances of authentic learning do occur. In order to overcome this problem, African educators need to embrace a wholesale change from teacher-centered to student-centered methods of learning. This way, teachers can introduce authentic learning methods in primary grades so that students become exposed to these methods throughout their education.

In addition to the interviews with Makerere professors, the personal experience of my daughter, a brilliant thirteen-year old girl, provides a vivid and realistic description that hits home. My story of SSA education rendered in the first chapter, where I experienced elementary school nearly twenty-five years ago, was freshly revived upon reading about a recent homework assignment that my daughter shared with me, transporting me back in time and hitting me with the hard reality that the teaching approaches in SSA countries, such as Uganda and Rwanda have experienced little if any change.

My daughter moved to Canada in 2013. Before she moved, she had attended school in Uganda from Kindergarten to Grade 5. Now in Grade 9, she attends Jean Forest Girls Leadership Academy, one of the Catholic schools in Edmonton, Alberta. As a parent, I have always helped my children with their homework and listened to them while they discussed their learning for the day. In 2015, my daughter told me about an activity that her class performs every morning: writing a letter to an imaginary friend discussing a topic of their choice. She asked me to read through her assignment responses. As I was going through them, I paused on a letter my daughter had written to Joy, her imaginary friend. The content of this letter touched my heart, as the very details that Melissa had shared with Joy recounted the experiences that I had faced in school. The following excerpt provides a snippet of her experiences while studying in Uganda:

> My country allowed spanking at school. Most teachers take that for granted and spank the hell out of kids. We children don't listen; we are notorious and disturbing and that's what makes kids. When we don't hand in our homework on time and you get spanked for it, some of us have reasons. What if we don't get the subject, or something? Can you blame us? No! Africa might have the worst teaching ever known because they don't teach because they like it, it's for the money. It is always money, money and more money. So, if you tell me that everyone is treated equal, does 'everyone' not include kids? We need to be taught because we are the future. Most importantly we need to be taught by people who really care about our education. (M. Muganga, personal communication, June 15, 2015)

Based on my research, my daughter's letter reflects the experiences and perceptions of children studying not only in Uganda but also throughout most of Africa, especially SSA. Most poignantly, the letter demonstrates that the same painful experience that I endured while pursuing my education in the 1980s has continued throughout the decades since. Just as I received caning multiple times from my teachers, my daughter, an entire generation later, still experienced the same harsh disciplinary methods. By understanding African education from the perspective of a student, who called it "the worst teaching ever known," the desperate need for transformation becomes apparent.

Although the letter of an adolescent girl provides a snapshot of the elementary school system in SSA, eerily similar methods and experiences occur at the postsecondary level. In my doctoral study, one of the professors recounted that, in his experience as a member of a school board, he had witnessed teachers beating young girls with a cane. This experience led him to question the very nature of education:

> During this time, I ... noticed that teachers were giving corporal punishment to the students. This gave me the feeling that we got it wrong; we do not understand what education is. These learners were adolescents. I told the teachers that these adolescents have issues and that maybe nobody is willing to listen to them and all you do is cane them in response. By caning maturing girls, what do you teach them? Personally, I think that education in Africa, especially Uganda, has a long way to go because it was ill-conceived. (P. Ssenkusu, personal communication, April 20, 2017)

This interview, which occurred in the early part of 2017, demonstrates the harsh reality that the caning I had experienced over twenty-five years ago still occurs in elementary classrooms within SSA schools. The professor's repeated insistence that "we do not understand what education is," shows the dire need for improvement not only in teaching methods but also in many aspects of education.

THE NEED FOR CHANGE

This chapter has highlighted the desperate need for changes in SSA education systems from the perspective of both academic and personal sources. The need to rethink education is further echoed by the former Rwandan Minister for Education, Professor Silas Lwakabamba, while speaking at the opening of a three-day UNESCO – Africa Regional Conference. The minister announced his government's search for new solutions for the country's education system. Specifically, he argued that education needs to provide people with the understanding, competencies, and values that they require for addressing the many challenges that our societies and economies face (Mwai, 2015). In order to address Professor Lwakabamba's call for action, the many challenges present in African postsecondary institutions can be overcome by implementing authentic learning approaches that address the needs of the twenty-first century labor market. Juma (2014) alludes to the need to reinvent Africa's universities by eschewing the traditional system and embracing practices that trigger the growth of dynamic economies through entrepreneurship and innovation, which can occur through student-centered learning approaches. These methodologies allow students to create meaningful, useful, and shared outcomes from their learning that demonstrate relevance to the community (Mamdami, 2000). Hence, teachers need to embrace current technological modes in order to enhance the effectiveness of their instruction. The tradeoff between the desire to provide equal and universal access to education and the need for a higher quality of education can be overcome by incorporating authentic learning approaches (DFID, 2012). Consequently, the next chapter will discuss the current state of authentic learning in SSA.

CHAPTER FIVE
AUTHENTIC LEARNING IN SSA

Choose Learning that Makes Sense

MY STORY ABOUT MY OWN EXPERIENCE OF RABBIT farming and Saidi's weaving business represent rare instances of authentic learning in SSA, especially given the fact that the rest of the country – including my parents, my teacher, and my principal – all chastised me for my involvement with real-life learning. My teacher's insistence that I couldn't mix rabbit farming with school, my mother's declaration that my involvement with Saidi's business was "running my future," and my headmaster's administration of twenty-five lashes for skipping useless and irrelevant classroom lessons paints a bleak picture of how an entire society rejects practical learning opportunities that not only facilitate student learning but also bolster the nation's economy.

As discussed in the previous chapter, Africa still remains mired in an outdated, teacher-centered mode of education – an extreme example of what Revington (2016) and Robinson (2010) refer to as the "industrial" mode. Unfortunately, the reluctance of SSA nations to make wholesale changes to education has resulted in negative individual effects, as evidenced from my personal story in Chapter 1, and national effects, such as the skills gap that remain in many crucial industries. While other countries throughout the world have implemented various aspects of authentic learning, Africa lags behind both western and non-western nations. Although advanced schooling systems exist in parts of North America and Europe, such as the reformed Finnish system, a discussion of these systems exceed the scope of the book. However, some developing and underdeveloped non-western countries have begun to incorporate authentic learning opportunities both on a smaller and larger scale. These countries can ideally serve as an example or model for SSA nations to emulate in their efforts to implement authentic learning experiences despite obstacles that include limited resources and infrastructural challenges.

INTERNATIONAL EXAMPLES OF AUTHENTIC LEARNING

Despite their history of poverty, many countries in Asia and the Middle East have recently developed emerging economies due to the rapidly-accelerating phenomena of globalization and increasing trade relations with major world powers such as the United States. Consequently, the education systems of these nations have responded to these technological and economic changes. More than half of the students in South Asia currently enter secondary school (Watkins, 2013) showing the increased access that these students experience. In addition, the international prominence of the western world has influenced the education systems of eastern countries to adopt student-centered pedagogical methods (Humes, 2013). Although the use of western methods and technologies requires some caution due to the considerable differences in cultural values (King, 2011), developing countries can adapt these approaches to align with their ideological beliefs. A study by Westbrook et al. (2013) found that in developing countries, teachers' communication strategies facilitated interactive teaching methods, which subsequently increased learning outcomes. This literature review discovered that teachers' positive attitudes towards their practice and their students provided them with the ideal mindset for utilizing interactive and communicative teaching tools in their classrooms. Some of these teaching practices included continual feedback, connections between theory and student experience, creation of a safe environment, cooperative learning tasks, use of real materials, effective use of student questioning, appropriate demonstrations and explanations, use of local languages, and changes in lesson sequences (Westbrook et al., 2013). These examples, which demonstrate that countries with limited resources can still utilize student-centered learning approaches in an effective manner, could inspire SSA nations to change their methods accordingly.

Among the active or student-centered teaching methodologies, authentic learning has been partially incorporated in Asian and Middle Eastern countries. When discussing the use of authentic learning in the United Arab Emirates, Zualkernan (2006) provides a unique framework that guides instructors in designing their own authentic learning initiatives rather than providing specific techniques or approaches. This framework includes pedagogical design, architectures, environmental context, and learning materials. In addition, he mentions various authentic learning experiences in the educational environment, including the student-centered approaches of problem-based learning, inquiry-based learning, role-play simulation, game-based learning, case study-based learning, and project-based learning, some of which were briefly discussed in Chapter 2. These various types of student-centered learning can interact and overlap with one another to provide at least some use of authentic learning in the classroom.

In terms of specific authentic learning methods and strategies, other studies show that teachers and instructors have begun to exploit the capabilities of information and communication technology to provide authentic learning experiences in a number of world regions. Safuan and Soh (2013) report on a Turkish initiative in which the implementation of authentic learning with social media supported students in developing analytical thinking, problem solving, and collaboration skills. Similarly, Neo, Neo, and Tan (2012) found that the use of technology complemented student-centered learning by helping students to develop skills such as creativity and problem solving. These latter authors report that despite the initial results of such endeavors, which reveal optimistic student attitudes towards learning and improved academic results, teachers still lack the knowledge and confidence for designing technology-based learning environments for their students (Neo et al., 2012). Despite these setbacks, both investigations suggest that the use of authentic learning in Middle Eastern and Asian countries can help students to develop the real-world skills required by today's workforce. Focusing on mobile technology, Conejar and Kim (2014) investigate the way in which devices such as phones, tablets, e-readers, apps, and online learning platforms can improve educational access, equity, and quality on an international scale. These authors found that mobile technologies can help teachers by supporting their educational practice and improving lesson delivery as well as demonstrating student benefits. Despite the high cost of implementing such devices, the authors argue that these gadgets will continue to decrease in price, making them more affordable for less developed countries (Conejar & Kim, 2014). When the costs of mobile devices and other information and communication technology decreases, perhaps SSA nations can take advantage of their affordability as well as their support in providing authentic learning experiences.

SINGAPORE

Among all Asian nations, one of the more competitive education systems in the eastern part of the world belongs to Singapore. Unlike SSA, Singapore has discovered the importance of education as a source of competitive strength and economic growth as well as a way to spur technological change. In addition, the country has become privy to the emerging knowledge-based economy and the increasing need for intellectual capital in society (Tan, Wong, Gopinathan, Goh, & Wong, 2007). Singapore's Ministry of Education emphasizes the importance of teaching students twenty-first century skills (Meng, 2014), which relate to the creative economy, as discussed in the subsequent chapter. Singapore has recently implemented student-centered and constructivist learning principles, leading to the incorporation of authentic and experiential learning (Knobloch, 2003) not only as isolated initiatives but also as part of their wholesale methodological changes to the delivery of education.

In fact, Singapore has realized the necessity of connecting education to work. Meng (2014) discusses the Applied Learning Programme (ALP), which facilitates the delivery of authentic learning in Singapore schools by providing students with "real world" experiences (p. 1). This realistic learning provides students with cross-curricular experiences that relates their knowledge to the practical world (Meng, 2014). In conjunction with ALP, the work-integrated learning (WIL) program teaches students modern competencies that they need to acquire for their career by fostering twenty-first century skills such as collaboration, communication, and problem solving. Some of the learning activities and assessment approaches involve research projects, reflective journaling, conference presentations, supervisor evaluation, case studies, portfolios, teamwork, discussion board evaluation, and facilitator meetings (Meng, 2014). Ti, Tan, Khoo, and Chen (2006) investigated the use of simulation training as a means of providing active participation and realistic scenario-based practice for medical students. The results of this study revealed that learners practicing with simulations performed more effectively than those observing (Ti et al., 2006). The promising strides made by Singapore as well as the isolated examples from other Asian countries provide a positive precedent for SSA nations to implement both individual and systematic changes that facilitate the introduction of student-centered learning principles, and, more specifically, authentic learning.

AUTHENTIC LEARNING IN SSA

As compared to other nations, African countries have been slow to implement authentic learning in their classrooms, one reason for the paucity of studies investigating authentic learning in SSA. In the past decade, the educational policies in several African nations have begun to mandate the use of interactive learning approaches in the classroom at all levels of education (Vavrus et al., 2011). Despite these mandates, the efforts to incorporate authentic learning at the postsecondary level have lagged behind those in other nations; many of these initiatives have proven fragmented and ineffective. A report by the United Nations (2011) suggested that African nations could learn from the experiences of developed and developing countries regarding the implementation of authentic learning, as discussed above with Singapore. Additionally, researchers have recommended that teachers and educators in African schools and institutions use open educational resources (European Commission, 2014; Hogan, Carlson, & Kirk, 2015). Hogan et al. (2015) describe open educational resources as those that can be shared or copied free of charge; in addition, teachers or instructors can revise the resources to deliver their own customized material. These resources represent ideal learning materials in African countries not only because of their easy access and inexpensive cost but also because they encourage authentic learning practices by enabling students and teachers to collaborate, engage in critical thinking, and innovate (Hogan et al., 2015). Another inexpensive means of learning involves project-based learning, where students initiate their own learning through inquiry and work collaboratively with others. This method of learning represents an inexpensive means of obtaining experience with technology as well as gaining problem solving and communication skills (Bell, 2010). Despite these few suggestions, African nations still require a more systematic approach for incorporating authentic learning in postsecondary classrooms.

Despite the barriers mentioned in the preceding chapter and illuminated again in Chapter 8, an extensive review of the literature highlights several isolated examples of authentic learning that have occurred in SSA nations. In some instances, instructors have used authentic learning to teach foreign languages. The teaching of languages assumes prime importance in SSA, especially since African universities recruit students from a wide variety of cultural and linguistic backgrounds (Titus, 2013). In one study, Alidou et al. (2006) discuss the implementation of bilingual language education in SSA. These authors propose curricular revisions that enable African students to learn their native languages as well as the dominant European language, such as English or French. Specifically, they suggest that the use of authentic multilingual language models in schools will increase the return on investments in education as well as boost the social and economic development of SSA countries (Alidou et al., 2006). Similarly, Motlhaka (2014) discusses an authentic learning technology-based initiative that addressed the teaching and learning of English as a Second Language (ESL). The authors found that the authentic learning experience provided students with access to information and a community audience outside of the classroom as well as enhanced students' awareness of themselves as legitimate participants in a labor market (Motlhaka, 2014). Both of these studies address the importance of authentic learning in teaching students the essential soft skills required for the labor market in today's creative economy, as further discussed in the next chapter.

In addition to scholarly research, interviews with Ugandan professors illustrate that a few attempts at authentic learning have begun to occur within SSA universities. A few professors at Uganda's Makerere University mention that they attempt to implement some form of student-centered learning through class presentations, which divide students into groups and make each group responsible for researching, learning, and presenting their assigned topic to the class. In particular, one professor mentioned that he provides realistic challenges or problems to his master's students as a way of preparing them for real-life scenarios that they may face in their job:

> I require my students to examine real life situations, challenges, or problems, like curriculum-related problems. Then, they conduct research about these problems; this task has been very helpful. For instance, if a student is an administrator in a school or is teaching economics, then I require them to identify gaps in the curriculum. (C. Mugimu, personal communication, April 28, 2017)

Another professor mentioned that although he still mainly uses the lecture method, he has made occasional attempts to integrate what he terms "interactive methods" in the classroom through group work, discussion, and even field work:

> We have other methods that are interactive, where our students are involved in activities. Even when we are teaching, we engage the students in teaching and learning. We give them assignments and encourage them to work together as a group for doing presentations ... we emphasize the practical aspects with the students, such as going into the field, sitting with them, showing them, and discussing things. (S.W. Wafula, personal communication, April 20, 2017)

One of these interactive methods involves the use of storytelling:

> Usually, when new students come, we provide them with as many illustrations as possible from their own school experiences. They retell these examples, and some of these instances are so fresh. We see everybody connecting, and they have so many stories. We want them to tell us as many stories as they can. I think this practice links more directly to the world than in the past, where we gave students so many examples about ourselves. (P. Ssenkusu, personal communication, April 20, 2017)

As you can see, these experiences of telling stories not only allow students to make sense of their personal experiences but also enable them to connect with one another. Despite the growing awareness of the need to connect theory to practice in school, this professor was the only interview participant who mentioned taking his students into the field as a way of providing a realistic element to their classroom learning. Although examples like these do exist, they are few and far between, concealed by the predominant focus on teacher-centered learning methods.

Scholarly research has attested to the benefits of using authentic learning in SSA classrooms. Specifically, the use of authentic learning in SSA has shown to not only improve learning outcomes for students but also to increase teacher or student-teacher competencies. Rowe, Bozalek, and Frantz (2013) discussed the way in which instructors can effectively use technology to create meaningful experiences for students. Specifically, these authors suggest that educators should provide students with open access to platforms that allow them to meaningfully and independently construct their own knowledge rather than merely using technology to reinforce dominant, expert-based knowledge. The result of such efforts assists students in developing real-world skills, such as critical thinking, that will support them in the working world (Rowe et al., 2013). Bozalek et al. (2013) conducted a survey of 265 higher educators in South Africa that claim to use authentic learning technologies. Although the respondent reports demonstrated that the precise usage and effectiveness differed substantially among the participants, one common theme throughout the study emphasized the importance of emerging technologies in facilitating authentic learning opportunities (Bozalek et al., 2013). While many African nations struggle with resource limitations, the benefits of technology-mitigated authentic learning opportunities should encourage stakeholders to maximize these strategies.

Authentic learning opportunities should benefit teachers as well as students, especially since teachers need to develop and grow their practice. Focusing on educators rather than students, Zwiers (2007) implemented a teacher-training program in Ethiopia that emphasized the development of active learning methods and assessments in areas of limited resources. In addition, this program enabled teachers to engage in critical reflection about the effectiveness of various teaching ideas and practices. The results of the study indicated that authentic and personalized learning methods enhanced the effectiveness of student learning through the active engagement in realistic topics. In addition, this pedagogical approach provided greater benefits to both students and teachers in using performance-based assessments and promoted the necessary involvement in traditional and community home education practices (Zwiers, 2007). The success of this investigation demonstrates the need for other SSA regions to incorporate similar studies in both teacher training and student education programs. Benefits of authentic learning, not only in SSA but also throughout the world, are expounded upon in Chapter 7.

LOW TECHNOLOGY APPROACHES

Due to the paucity of resources and limited infrastructural capabilities in SSA countries, teachers and instructors need to exercise creativity in devising authentic learning experiences that utilize the available resources while minimizing expenditures. Specifically, SSA universities can learn from the examples of inexpensive authentic learning provided in the western world. Hein (1999) discusses the value of field trips to locations like museums, while Szczepanski (2006) supports the use of environmental or outdoor education in providing authentic learning experiences for students. Similarly, Higgins and Nicol (2002) advocate for the use of outdoor learning as a means of teaching students about the environment while simultaneously providing them with realistic learning experiences. These approaches can extend to SSA nations, where outdoor or field-based activities allow teachers to engage students in the community without incurring significant expenditures or relying on technology. Although these initiatives may require transportation and hence depend on the availability of vehicles to take students to remote locations, students can access some nearby communities that are within walkable distance or even in the schoolyard. In discussing the student-centered approach of problem-based learning, explained in Chapter 2, Wilson (1996) mentions the use of realistic problems that refer to actual issues in Africa, such as political conflict or mining corruption, while Moos and Honkomp (2014) discuss the phenomenon of adventure learning, where students can explore real-life issues by engaging in adventures such as climbing Mt. Kilimanjaro. The provision of field trips to cultural heritage sites in SSA cities can even serve as authentic learning experiences; one Makerere University professor reported that some of the students in his institution "go and participate in what they call fieldwork in geography. They go out there to learn, and in history, they go to visit those cultural sites" (M. B. Mulumba, personal communication, April 20, 2017). Along with my personal experience of animal husbandry, these field trips represent an inexpensive way of teaching students about the real world. In conjunction, these experiences represent authentic learning activities that instructors can implement to overcome resource limitations in SSA countries.

Another type of authentic learning involving minimal technological resources can focus on improving communities. The new phenomenon of service-based learning, originating in North America, can apply to African countries, especially given the extent of poverty in these nations. Reed (2015) reports that students increasingly seek jobs based around social issues, such as non-profit corporations. In order to address this need, Smith (2015) suggests the provision of community service jobs for students. Some initiatives have already embraced this idea by providing service-based learning into their curriculum. For example, Mariappan, Monemi, and Fan (2005) examined a specific case study of service learning, a community-based application of constructivism that relates classroom material to community issues in an engineering class. These authors found that this experience represented an effective instructional approach that provided students with a realistic means of addressing complex social problems. Students in the study gained additional knowledge as well as concrete insights into issues in their field (Mariappan et al., 2005). Lawrence, Harvey, McKnight, and Block (2016) discuss the idea of increasing the power of neighborhoods through an asset-based approach to increasing social capital. This method seeks to empower individual citizens as a means of enhancing capacity-building within the neighborhood and foster connections between neighbors as a means of developing neighborhood-based economies. The benefits of this approach include greater networks within communities, reduced dependence on the service-based economy, enhanced well-being of the neighborhood, and financial savings (Lawrence et al., 2016). These low-tech authentic experiences not only provide students with realistic community experiences but also help students to devise solutions for poverty.

Furthermore, other studies demonstrate the ability to utilize limited technological resources for implementing authentic learning. Similar to Bozalek et al., (2013), Kandiero and Jagero (2014) proposed the use of emerging technologies to teach a business mathematics undergraduate course at Africa University in Zimbabwe. These authors found that this approach increased students' motivation to learn; however, the authors failed to address the full impact of the methodology due to time limitations. Similarly, Jaffer et al. (2007) argued that even in cases of limited resources, African countries can implement various types of technological interventions designed to provide authentic learning opportunities for students. For example, these authors suggested the use of Excel-based spreadsheets for developing mathematical literacy. In her conference paper, Campbell (2013) investigated the effects of providing students in a first-year mathematics class with access to a database of multi-language video explanations. She found that students that had access to the videos experienced improved examination results (Campbell, 2013). Lastly, Barnes, Gachago, and Ivala (2012) conducted an investigation that assessed the effectiveness of digital storytelling as an effective assessment method in a South African university. The results of the study demonstrated that while the authentic learning technology of digital storytelling increased student engagement and motivation, additional research needs to examine the level of support required for students to successfully develop a finished product (Barnes et al., 2012). Another potential problem with this approach involves the fact that digital technologies are used to replace rather than supplement student literacy, thus contributing to the declining literacy levels in postsecondary education (Wesley, 2016). Nevertheless, these investigations show that universities and instructors in SSA nations can utilize even slightly outmoded technological resources or "low-tech" resources to provide students with authentic learning opportunities, thus bolstering their learning outcomes.

HIGH TECHNOLOGY APPROACHES

In addition to using low-technology approaches, SSA instructors can take advantage of more recent technology when available. This more modern technology includes the use of smartphones, tablets, and personal computers along with the internet and its various platforms. Traxler and Deardon (2005) conducted a pilot study that aimed to use SMS mobile technology to support teacher education in SSA. Specifically, this project developed a distance-based learning program that reduced the geographic isolation of learners and delivered education in a cost-effective and sustainable way. Although the results of the project are inconclusive, they nevertheless raise many promising opportunities for enhancing learning and communication at all levels as well as fostering greater connections between students, teachers, technologists, educationalists, and policy-makers in SSA. Some of the suggested delivery methods include conferences, content delivery, links, reminders, access to learning resources, and asynchronous conversations among students and teachers (Traxler & Deardon, 2005). Another investigation involved the use of interactive radio as a means of delivering authentic learning experiences to increase the equality of educational access. The study found that this method increased learning opportunities for students in disadvantaged groups, including those with learning disabilities as well as those in remote geographical regions (Simpson, 2013).

The use of the internet for educational support has only become prominent for the last two decades, with most African countries lagging behind in its usage. One instructor at Makerere University revealed that he uses an online learning platform entitled "ED Model," to facilitate discussion amongst students (C. Mugimu, personal communication, April 28, 2017), while another professor has experimented with Google Docs as a way of creating interaction (M. B. Mulumba, personal communication, April 20, 2017). Both instructors revealed that the students enjoyed the opportunity to interact with other students, not only increasing their motivation to learn but also strengthening their collaborative learning abilities, an essential skill in today's creative economy. In the literature, Damoense (2003) recognized the key role of the internet in shifting from conventional, teacher-centered modes to more student-friendly approaches such as authentic learning, recommending that instructors of higher learning implement this tool in an effective way. Finally, Titus (2013) discussed the use of wikis and blogs in mediating authentic learning opportunities in Africa, arguing that such tools can transform educators' approach to teaching while improving student outcomes through facilitating collaboration, enhancing digital literacy, and increasing student engagement. Although these studies demonstrate that some educational researchers have successfully showed the effective use of authentic and personalized learning in the classrooms of postsecondary SSA institutions, such efforts have been fragmented and require wholesale changes rather than isolated examples.

Postsecondary education in Africa recently began to adopt models of online education that have been implemented throughout the western world. One of the more recent trends involved with personalized learning, a subset of authentic learning, involves the rise of online learning courses and universities. For example, Massive Open Online Courses (MOOCs), which are affiliated with many major North American universities, provide students with open access and unlimited participation in all aspects of the course. Students can access course resources, assignments, and grades online while interacting with instructors and classmates through discussion forums, email, and chat features. While most major universities in North America and other western countries offer some of their courses or programs online, other institutions have established their niche as online universities or colleges. For example, Athabasca University in Alberta, Canada not only functions as an independent institution offering solely online courses but also allows students to combine their courses with those of other universities (Athabasca University, 2017). Other examples of these internet-based higher education programs include edX, Coursera, iTunes U, Open2Study, Udacity and Udemy (Ruff, 2016; Wheeler, 2016). In addition, an online computer programming and design school, Thinkful, allows students to learn work-ready skills with the assistance of one-on-one mentors (Thinkful, 2016). The flexibility offered by these types of programs allow students to learn at their own time, place, and pace, while enhancing educational equity. This flexibility widens the demographic groups that can access university education, including adult learners, distance learners, individuals with disabilities, and international students (Bountrogianni, 2015). In particular, online courses broaden the access for international students, which, according to recent reports, are growing strongly in Canadian universities (Contact North, 2015). *New African Magazine* (2017) reveals the first African online university, The African Virtual University (2017), which originated in 1997. Funded by the World Bank, this initiative has since graduated over 60,000 students across the continent and represented an isolated example of attempts to utilize new technology while improving educational equity and access (New African, 2017).

Despite the promising potential represented by many of these studies, an undercurrent of caution remains regarding the implementation of authentic learning in

SSA nations. In addition to the limitations discussed in the final chapter of this book, other potential problems exist in misapplying authentic learning in the environment of African universities. Teachers' lack of training, mentioned in the final chapter, may influence them to employ technology-based authentic learning for the wrong reasons, including personal convenience, administrative pressure, and the promise of increased student motivation. Herrington and Kervin (2007) suggest that teachers follow theoretical guidelines in their implementation of authentic learning initiatives. In order to avoid this pitfall, teachers can utilize theoretical "checklists" or guidelines to ensure that the learning experiences they choose to implement embrace the principles of authentic learning. Two of the more noted approaches in the literature include the twelve elements listed by Revington (2016) as discussed in Chapter 2, and Herrington's Nine Principles of Authentic Learning. Specifically, Herrington's principles include the following: 1) authentic context, 2) authentic tasks and activities, 3) access to expert performances, 4) multiple roles and perspectives, 5) collaborative construction of knowledge, 6) reflection on abstractions, 7) articulation to enable tacit knowledge, 8) coaching and scaffolding, and 9) authentic assessment (Herrington, Parker, & Boase-Jelinek, 2014). In addition to principles, other authors have provided guidelines for teachers to develop their own approaches. For instance, Zualkernan (2006) provides a theoretical framework that teachers and instructors can follow in devising their own versions of authentic learning. Other authors, such as Rowe et al. (2013), offer studies showing examples of effective authentic learning activities that teachers can implement. Although these studies are limited in their application and reach, they represent a promising start for educators in SSA to emulate their teaching. The next chapter, Chapter 6, discusses the creative economy and suggests that systems of education around the world, including that of SSA, adopt their approaches to adequately prepare students for the changing workforce.

CHAPTER SIX
THE CREATIVE ECONOMY

Bringing Ideas to Life

BACK IN THE 1980S AND 1990S, THE TERM "THE CRE-ative economy" had not yet come into existence. As a student during those years, I would never have dreamed of mixing those two words. The connection between my education and my aspired career path in the field of economics was anything but creative; I had perceived it as a straight and predictable line through primary, secondary, and tertiary education. I had envisioned that this linear model of education, which Ken Robinson mentions in his TED Talks, would be followed by a linear career model in which, as a freshly-graduated student, I started at the bottom and worked my way to the top until retirement. My Canadian colleague conceived her educational and career journey in much the same way. As a naturally creative person who excelled in the arts and humanities, she sought a career in which she could use her talents but struggled to find traction in the business world. When she first learned about the creative economy, she wished that it had existed during her undergraduate tenure and that someone had been there to show her the possibilities. She felt torn between choosing an office job she hated and pursuing her dream, albeit from the confines of a studio apartment and with a bus pass. Even today, many secondary and postsecondary students remain unaware of the possibilities offered by the creative economy.

Before transitioning towards a solid definition of the creative economy, we will first revisit the purposes of education, mentioned earlier in the book. As demonstrated in Chapter 2, philosophies of education have largely reflected the purposes and structure of society. One of the major aims of education has always been to prepare students for society, including economic, social, and political functioning. In reflecting upon the 1963 Robbins Report, Anderson (2010) highlighted that schools, especially universities, had four main purposes: 1) to provide instruction in skills; 2) to promote general powers of the mind that produce intelligent students; 3) to maintain research alongside teaching; and 4) to transmit a common culture and standards of citizenship (Anderson, 2010). With the evolution of society, these purposes have arguably been expanded into the need to prepare students for the labor market (Contact North, 2015). Unfortunately, universities have failed to adapt to the modern economy despite substantial changes over the last several decades (Charbonneau, 2009), resulting in what Ken Robinson refers to as a "crisis of human resources" (Robinson, 2010) throughout the world. Accordingly, this chapter will discuss the dire need for fundamental change at the level of postsecondary education in order to provide a greater alignment between education and the workforce while preparing students for the creative economy.

LAWRENCE MUGANGA

EDUCATION IN A TRANSFORMING SOCIETY

As discussed throughout various portions of this book, prior to the twenty-first century, the education system prepared students for life in an industrial-based manufacturing economy. The initial transformation of the formal schooling system began during the Industrial Revolution, in the late nineteenth century, where labor became increasingly specialized. Educational philosophies reflected this change, as John Dewey's original version of constructivism, discussed in Chapter 2, taught students "hard knowledge" of facts or subject areas (Dobbin, 2009). In addition, philosophical writings such as Emile Durkheim's *Division of Labor* called for changes in the organization of all aspects of society, including the education system (Dobbin, 2009). Based on the shifting ideologies in society, schools provided students for employment in factories, reflecting the same structure, values, and attributes that manufacturing workers required. This approach, which Revington (2016) and others term the "classic industrial age approach" (para. 4), fostered obedience in students through the necessity of following rules, taking turns, sitting quietly, and heeding instructions. In fact, the two stories presented at the beginning of the book contain instances of this very aspect. The compartmentalization of education further reflected the factory life, which pigeonholed workers into a single station or task. Correspondingly, schools segmented subjects into separate areas and timetabled students' learning (Revington, 2016), reflecting the importance of order, structure, and scheduling in the manufacturing economy. This new organization of society, economy, and education departed drastically from the holistic Indigenous perspective that viewed trades, and, by extension, education, as phenomenon involving many aspects, tasks, and functions.

The plethora of problems with this industrial modality of education have been poignantly illustrated in Chapter 1 through a variety of sources, including personal experience, academic research, and even the entertainment industry, which, in fitting with the creative economy, echoes the messages of famous educators throughout the world. The biggest failure of this mass-produced, teacher-centered, one-size-fits-all brand of education involves the pitiful waste of talent. As Prince EA (2016) states, "if you judge a fish based on its ability to climb a tree, it will go its whole life believing that its stupid." Unfortunately, this is exactly what the education system has done to squander children's talents and leave them ill-prepared for the labor market. In fact, even Paul McCartney never enjoyed music class and his teacher never told him that he had musical talent (Peritz, 2017). While the disastrous effects of the industrialized education system have already ruined many students throughout the world, the emergence of the creative economy emphasizes the urgent need for greater change that aligns schools more closely with the real world.

THE CREATIVE ECONOMY

Imagine a world in which, rather than trudging to work with your aching body barely aware enough to comprehend the reality of a long, grueling eight-hour workday filled with activities and people you have increasingly grown to despise, you can get that coveted extra hour of sleep, wake up feeling refreshed and anxious to begin your exciting workday from the comfort of home where you do what you love. It sounds like some sort of fairy tale, perhaps concocted from the overwrought brain of a person who spends many hours chained to a desk, slowly losing their luster for life and perhaps their sanity. However, the unfortunate reality is that the first scenario, the grueling workday we despise, applies to most of us. To quote Ken Robinson (2010), people "endure rather than enjoy" what they do for a living. So much for the dream of loving what you do.

But wait. It's not a dream, or at least it doesn't necessarily have to be. While some postsecondary students may, in fact, want to participate in the manufacturing or production-based economy, they shouldn't as if this is the only option for their future. In recent years, the economies in the countries of the western world have evolved from a resource-based or manufacturing market for which this industrial age school system adequately prepared students to a knowledge-based economy, which focuses on "the production and distribution of knowledge and information, rather than the production and distribution of things" (Sawyer, 2008, p. 2). The primary element for this new economic paradigm involves the aspect of creativity. Ken Robinson defined creativity as "the process of having original ideas that have value" (Strauss, 2015). Robinson further argues that most people misunderstand the concept of creativity, largely associating this word with skills in the arts, such as drawing, singing, dancing, and acting. However, as Robinson elaborates, creativity is not a process or an innate talent that you either possess or lack, but it is a "process" which people can learn and improve (Strauss, 2015). In addition, he asserts that creativity goes beyond the arts; in fact, creativity can permeate any subject, industry, or area of life, including even sciences, math, and technology. As shown by the examples of animal husbandry and weaving innovations in my personal story, creativity is an essential element of any business venture.

Burgeoning awareness about the important role of creativity in the business world has led to the creation of the term "creative economy." Howkins (2001) arguably first coined the term, describing the twenty-first century, knowledge-based economy as "the creative economy," which signifies an increasing tendency towards economic transactions that involve the creation and dissemination of innovative products. Several industries typically generate creative products, including advertising, architecture, art, crafts, design, fashion, film, games, information and communication technology, music, performing arts, publishing, research, software, toys, TV, and video games (Howkins, 2001). Initially, the creative economy was commonly perceived as encompassing mainly the artistic industries. The World Economic Forum (2016) describes the creative economy as a "sector" (p. 3), thus implying that it constitutes a single industry rather than permeating the entire economy. For instance, Goulet, Charles, and Triplett (2016) define the twelve creative industry clusters as comprising the following: advertising, architecture, agencies, creative technology, cultural heritage, design, fashion, film/broadcasting, writing/publishing, music, performing arts, and visual arts. An East African Report defines six creative industries in Africa as literary arts, performing arts, visual arts, media arts, cultural heritage, and design (Hivos, 2016). However, Schlesinger (2016) maintains that the innovativeness inherent in the so-called "creative" industries has spilled over into the more traditional sectors, including politics and business. The creative economy combines and exploits several trends in modern society, including information and communication technology, multiculturalism, and innovation in order to highlight the importance of shared knowledge, intellectual property rights, and new niches in the workforces (United Nations, 2015). Along with creating new niches in traditional industries, the creative economy has also witnessed a substantial rise in entrepreneurship.

An offshoot of the creative economy, a new phenomenon known as "the sharing economy," has allowed ordinary people to become entrepreneurs. Like the creative economy, the sharing economy focuses on starting with small clusters of people in local communities and gradually expanding into worldwide companies or industries. The sharing economy comprises a network of peer-to-peer services that regular citizens can offer directly to other people, usually local but sometimes in other parts of the country or even the world, in need of such services. These marketed services can range across a broad array of industries, include accommodation, transportation, and housekeeping. Some of the more famous companies that originated as peer-to-peer services include Airbnb, Uber, and Lyft (O'Reilly, 2015). These services, which harness modern information and communication technology, allow individuals to earn additional income with assets that they already possess, including vehicles or vacation homes (Israel, 2017). Although the sharing economy lacks wholesale innovation, it still requires people to create and market a product or service and requires sellers to exploit or exchange their assets in a thoughtful way to earn money. The peer-to-peer economy aligns closely with the idea of community capacity building, which creates small, local networks of individuals buying, selling, and exchanging products and services (Lawrence et al., 2016). In both of these types of small-scale economies, capacity building requires empowerment, which involves "equipping people with skills and competencies that they would not otherwise have" and "promoting people's ability to take responsibility for identifying and meeting their own and other people's needs" (Craig, 2006, p. 11). This approach takes a bottom-up rather than a top-down approach by empowering the individual and then building outwards into neighborhoods and cities.

Due to its emphasis on the importance of knowledge and information as a type of product, this creative economy requires higher-order thinking skills that focus on the manipulation of information, including problem solving, critical thinking, communication, collaboration, analysis, and innovation (Barron & Darling-Hammond, 2008; Revington, 2016; Sawyer, 2008). Sawyer (2008), who vouches for the necessity of rethinking education in light of the knowledge-based economy, explains many of these skills in his article. Based on the shifting economy, he insists that the "memorization of facts and procedures is not enough for success" (p. 4). Revington (2016) concurs with Sawyer, arguing that memorization uses only three percent of a student's brain capacity. Rather, students require "a deep conceptual understanding of complex concepts, and the ability to work with them creatively to generate new ideas, new theories, new products, and new knowledge" (Sawyer, 2008, p. 4). The knowledge of "complex concepts" corresponds to critical thinking and analysis, while the manipulation of such ideas to generate new aspects refers to innovation and creativity (Revington, 2016). Furthermore, Sawyer defines communication as the ability "to express [oneself] clearly both verbally and in writing" (p. 4), and synthesis as the capacity to "learn integrated and usable knowledge" (p. 4). In addition, he defines problem solving or reasoning as a skill that requires an individual to hold a mental representation of a problem and thoroughly examine solutions until reaching the ideal goal. Finally, Sawyer discusses the importance of collaboration, or working effectively with others, arguing that students learning in pairs or groups gain more knowledge than students learning in isolation from one another (Sawyer, 2008). These essential skills, which not only align with the knowledge-based or creative economy but also constitute the "soft skills" that allow graduates to transfer from one job or career to another, are best developed through student-centered learning methodologies, especially that of authentic learning. These skills, and their association with both authentic learning and the creative economy, will undergo further discussion throughout the remainder of the book.

EFFECTS OF THE CREATIVE ECONOMY

As part of the creative economy, knowledge has undergone a conceptual transformation. Rather than a static idea, knowledge represents a process that occurs between an individual and his or her surrounding environment (Sawyer, 2008). As a result, graduates and employees need to acquire more than the memorization of facts; they require the ability to manipulate complex concepts by way of critical thinking and innovation. Education systems throughout the world require wholesale revision to address these needs and prepare graduates for the "real world" and their prospective careers (Sawyer, 2008), which may change frequently throughout their lifetimes. In fact, Choise (2016) suggests that today, adults may change their careers as often as seven times, which makes the acquisition of transferable "soft" or "creative" skills important. While previous schooling models trained students with the hard skills required for specific vocations, today's fluid economy requires students to learn "soft" skills that can apply to all professions. Schlesinger (2016) reports that in Britain, higher education has begun to adapt to the creative economy, with several UK universities offering courses and degrees in creative and cultural industries; however, he argues that such programs ultimately oversupply the market with underpaying jobs in traditionally creative industries such as the arts. From this perspective, it is apparent that universities need to make wholesale changes in the way that they deliver education rather than simply creating new courses.

In addition to its new way of envisioning knowledge, the creative economy also places an enhanced emphasis on culture, especially given the recent emergence of a globalized economy. In fact, one of the objectives of higher education stipulated in the Robbins Report highlights the preservation of cultural values (Anderson, 2010; Robinson, 2013). Turpin (2015) argues that Canadian universities need to reflect the democratic values of society, including "intellectual integrity, freedom of inquiry and expression, and the equal rights and dignity of all persons" (para. 3). While reinforcing the cultural values of the home country, however, universities should also teach students about international or even globalized culture, especially given the prominence of multiculturalism in many societies worldwide. The United Nations and its affiliated organizations have been working to ensure that culture assumes an increased role in the economy worldwide (United Nations, 2013). The growing importance of culture has stimulated the creative economy, as universities have increasingly offered study abroad programs that teach students about various cultures of other countries (Havergal, 2016). Within this vision, the cultural industries of all countries have been recognized for their role in driving the economy and producing new ideas through innovative technologies. Specifically, the creative economy aims to create new businesses and jobs, generate income for people and industries, and develop exports (United Nations, 2013). Due to its global focus, the creative economy aims to create collaborative relationships among industries and even nations, forming new connections between different industrial sectors and countries in order to enhance revenue generation (United Nations, 2013). In addition to its financial benefits, the creative economy also provides non-monetary advantages, such as the development of social and cultural aspects as well as environmental and heritage preservation. These benefits increase individual quality of life and overall wellbeing through important relationships and increased cultural engagement (United Nations, 2013).

Several studies have linked the creative economy to the growing trend towards globalization. According to the Levin Institute (2015), globalization is "a process of interaction and integration among the people, companies, and governments of different nations" (para. 1). Globalization, like the creative economy, applies to many broad fields of study, including communication, business, and social sciences. The phenomenon of globalization, driven by advances in information technology and travel, has allowed people to learn about and directly experience different cultures and ethnicities (The Levin Institute, 2015). Globalization connects strongly to the creative economy through the movement towards specialization, where modern information and communication technologies facilitate the sharing of cultural knowledge. Not only does this new cultural information enhance the focus on knowledge but it also creates new niches in the market where new products and services can emerge. According to a United Nations report (2015), creative goods have spiked international trade in order to expand growth and development of economies worldwide, including those in developing nations. In turn, the globalized economy and the trend towards increasing specialization fosters entrepreneurial aspirations, as further discussed towards the end of this chapter. Havergal (2016) argues that universities and colleges must prepare students for an increasingly globalized world that will improve their chances of solving international problems. He suggests the provision of study-abroad experiences, where students travel to foreign countries to conduct learning activities that involve immersing themselves in the culture. In one such experience, students in a community development program travelled to Gambia to organize a business training center for youth, work in a women's rights center, or intern in a radio station (Havergal, 2016). These experiences not only provide students with practical experience but also broaden their concept of the world.

The creative economy contributes significantly to inclusiveness and cultural development throughout the world (United Nations, 2015). In Africa, the main region of interest in this book, the creative economy has undergone recent development. Africa contributes less than one percent to global creative exports due to limited resources (United Nations, 2013), thus showing that the culture industry in African countries remains largely untapped. However, African exports of creative goods have recently rose from $778 million in 2003 to $1900 million in 2012 (United Nations, 2015). Similar to the case with the education sectors, the cultural sectors in Africa face many challenges, including resource limitations, lack of trained or qualified personnel, infrastructural issues that limit distribution networks, lack of coordination among stakeholders, insulation within each guild or artistic association, low levels of artistic entrepreneurship, and decentralized governments that complicate unified policymaking. In particular, many policy makers resist linking culture to other industries, as they perceive culture as a luxury rather than an economic necessity in already financially struggling nations (United Nations, 2013; Hivos, 2016). Other broad, society-wide challenges implicit in East African culture include sexual and racial discrimination, government control of media, and lack of civil liberties embedded with the constitutions of these countries, thus quashing freedom and hence creativity (Hivos, 2016). The World Economic Forum (2016) provides suggestions for enhancing the creative economy in developing nations, which includes harnessing local strengths, enabling digital technology, inspiring entrepreneurs, stimulating government involvement, and the emphasizing the importance of locality.

Despite the lack of artistic entrepreneurship in Africa (Hivos, 2016), one emerging trend in many African nations involves the development of small, independent businesses that result from entrepreneurial efforts (United Nations, 2013). In fact, my own story back in Chapter 1 demonstrates the fact that even twenty or thirty years ago, children used their creativity to seek business opportunities, such as rabbit farming and weaving, as a way of overcoming the deficiencies of the education systems in SSA. However, similar to the case with graduates pursuing traditional employment, many African graduates seeking to create start-ups lack the necessary skills to succeed in businesses due to the lack of authentic learning opportunities within the education systems. The creation of start-ups requires many of the skills honed in authentic learning, including creativity, innovation, problem solving, decision making, and collaboration. Kampylis and Berki (2014) refer to these abilities as "creative thinking," which "enables students to apply their imagination to generating ideas, questions, and hypotheses, experimenting with alternatives, and evaluating their own and their peers' ideas, final products, and processes" (p. 6). According to these authors, creative thinking can be utilized in all levels and subject areas of education. Subsequent sections of this book will discuss the relationship between authentic learning and the creative economy, focusing explicitly on the way in which authentic learning adequately prepares students for living and working in the creative economy within their own culture as well as on an international and multicultural level.

The Need for Change in Higher Education

Despite the transformation of the economy from a manufacturing or production-based economy to a knowledge-based or creative economy, education systems, including those at the postsecondary level, have remained fixed in outdated structures and learning modes.

One of the problems preventing universities from transforming into institutions that foster creativity or provide practical, real-world experience involves the elitist mentality that has traditionally been associated with universities and Ivy League schools in particular. Specifically, universities have been historically envisioned as institutions for society's privileged elite, which traditionally comprised white, upper-class males (European Commission, 2014). One Ugandan professor echoes this sentiment, maintaining that in Africa, "there is a feeling that vocational education is for failures" (N. Itaaga, personal communication, April 20, 2017). This mindset, along with the increasingly inaccurate notion that universities represent the best path to a high-paying, well-respected career (Robinson, 2015), prevents universities from achieving genuine change. Even in Canada, one of the more modernized western countries, universities have lagged behind the knowledge-based economy due to its resource-intensive infrastructure (Florida & Spencer, 2015). In underdeveloped nations, such as SSA, universities remain even more resistant to change. Both academic and popular culture sources emphasize the outdated mentality that remains in educational systems around the world; Steve Revington, arguably the originator of authentic learning, argues that today's schools remain unchanged from over 150 years ago despite the profound changes that have occurred in society over that time span (Revington, 2016). Current students and recent graduates attest to the inadequacy of today's universities, with one student admitting that the postsecondary system reinforces "industrial repetition" (Harford, 2016, para. 5) and fails to challenge students to think outside of the box.

The inability or unwillingness of education to adapt to the creative economy represents a worldwide problem. In my personal interviews with Ugandan university instructors teaching at Makerere University, I discovered that most professors understand that the lecture method fails to provide students with the real-life skills needed in the creative economy. One of the instructors reported that during their school practice, the education "students have the content but cannot teach" (M. B. Mulumba, personal communication, April 20, 2017) at least according to their supervising teachers. Another professor states that although the goal of education involves preparing students for the labor market, "Here, there is mostly theory," which leads to large knowledge gaps between a student's education and the labor force demands (P. Ssenkusu, personal communication, April 25, 2017). Although Makerere University's education students, not unlike the education students in other parts of the world, attend practice teaching as part of their degree requirements, the quality of their practice teaching may not necessarily coincide with the expectations of the labor market. As admitted by a third instructor, "There are people that have been thinking that our students do not have skills" (S. W. Wafula, personal communication, April 20, 2017). The lack of high-quality and real-world skills that cater to the creative economy, even in professional programs, points to a massive failing of education in SSA.

The reluctance of education systems, and, more specifically, universities to adapt to the modern economy has resulted in several problems. The creative economy has witnessed a shift from stable, full-time employment in traditional corporate industries to other models of work, which include part-time work, temporary work, and entrepreneurship (Goulet et al., 2016). While the workforce, along with industries and specific employers, demand that students possess practical work experience along with the soft skills that require students to manipulate knowledge (Barron & Darling-Hammond, 2008), the schools requiring students to memorize isolated facts within the context of segmented subject areas that lack any connection with the real world (Revington, 2016). Shepard (2015) reports that only sixty percent of students within the traditional system of higher education find employment. Student surveys echo these sentiments, as many students who struggled to find a job immediately after graduation indicated their desire for more practical experiences or job-related skills. Some of the ways in which recent graduates request additional help include direct assistance from their university in finding work, the provision of workshops or seminars that enhance the students' professional skills, and the acquisition of more practical or job-related skills in their courses (Academia Group, 2016). Hewitt (2016) calls for stronger connections between postsecondary institutions and private sector employers.

In addition to the inability of higher education institutions to prepare students for the workforce, educational credentials have become devalued in society, leaving many new graduates unemployed or underemployed. This phenomenon, which my Canadian colleague experienced immediately upon graduating from her Bachelor of Arts program, known as credential inflation, involves the increasing reduction in the worth of postsecondary education degrees relative to the perceived demands of the labor market. Harford (2016) estimates that today's bachelor degree is roughly equivalent to yesterday's high school degree, which indicates the inadequacy of these undergraduate credentials for obtaining respectable employment. In North America, the proportion of the population with postsecondary education degrees has increased more rapidly than the proportion of available jobs, resulting in a workforce filled with overeducated and underemployed graduates (Vaisey, 2004; Van de Werfhorst & Anderson, 2005). The relative ineffectiveness of a bachelor degree has resulted in many students supplementing their education with postgraduate, professional, college, and technical degrees (Robinson, 2015; Van de Werfhorst & Anderson, 2005) In fact, Van Wyck (2016) points out that even graduate students with masters and doctorates struggle to find employment due to the diminishing job market and the tenure-track system. The proportion of employees with graduate degrees earning low wages has risen from 7.7 percent in 1997 to 12.4 percent in 2014 (Younglai, 2016). This inability of university graduates to find work deprives the economy of educated and potentially skilled workers, leading to the creation of a skills gap in many industries (Seidman, 2016). Arguably, the cause of credential inflation, in addition to the reason for skills gaps in the workforce, emanates from the inability of universities to provide students with the appropriate skills and experience that meets the needs of the creative economy.

Some sociologists maintain that credential inflation represents a type of capitalist control over society, where bureaucracies and governments exploit education systems to reproduce existing class structures (Tyler, 1982). From this perspective, credential inflation seems to comprise a type of backlash or countermeasure designed to maintain dominant class structures, where only elite members of the population have access to education. However, Levey and Lavin (2005) take a different viewpoint, contending that rising populations, along with easier access to education, has dramatically increased enrollment in universities. Since higher numbers of students have entered postsecondary educational institutions and received these once-coveted degrees, the perceived value of degrees has decreased, as they are now more readily available. This type of supply-and-demand explanation is echoed by Robinson (2015), who argues that today's universities feature "an oversupply of bachelor degree holders and an undersupply of entry-level work" (para. 5). Van de Werfhorst (2009) provides additional support for this viewpoint through his comparison of education to a marketplace commodity. When the value of education decreases, credential inflation increases the probability that students will pursue a university degree through the supply and demand mechanism. Taken together, these various explanations suggest that capitalist market structures tend to control education. Cote and Allahar (2008) argue that increasing enrolment and corresponding decreases in budgetary allowances per student lowers the quality of Canadian postsecondary education, thus accounting for the lower value of degrees. In addition, the diminished quality of education has prompted disengagement among professors and students, further lowering the quality and hence value of teaching and learning (Cote & Allahar, 2008). The phenomenon of credential inflation, arising from rising enrolment and lowered educational quality, leaves students poorly prepared and inadequately qualified for the job market.

Due to the gross misalignment between universities and workforce requirements, corporate jobs have become increasingly scarce, temporary, and uncertain, especially for new graduates (Shepard, 2015). Consequently, education systems, especially at the postsecondary level, require wholesale revisions to prepare graduates adequately for the contemporary creative economy while simultaneously mitigating the effect of credential inflation. Part of these changes indubitably involve the transformation and reorganization of universities, colleges, and technical institutes into institutions that align with the needs of the workforce by teaching students the essential twenty-first century skills and providing them with practical, job-related experience through the provision of internships, field placements, or practicums, all of which connect students to the real world and provide them with the job-ready experience that employers covet. Cote and Allahar (2008) suggest that institutions of higher learning restructure their curricula, programs, and courses to provide more practical, work-oriented programs along with fewer liberal arts degrees. However, a few recent initiatives have shown that arts and humanities degrees can successfully integrate with other departments as well as incorporate programs and activities that provide practical, real-world or work skills (Busl, 2015). In addition to preparing students for the real world of work, the provision of practical work experiences provides many benefits, including reduced classroom time, lower administrative expenditures, lower tuition fees, and increased market value of student degrees (Seidman, 2016). Although the number of practical work programs has increased over the past several years (Sherlock, 2016), these programs still require restructuring to accommodate a greater range of programs and courses. In fact, companies also benefit from internships, as, if used properly by the employer, student interns not only provide project assistance but also fresh ideas and the fulfillment of a commitment to corporate social responsibility by contributing to universities (Ricardo, 2015).

In addition to providing more work-based programs, universities need to cement the connection between classroom theory and practical experience. Resnick (1987) first proposed the idea of bridging apprenticeships, which connect theoretical learning in the classroom to the application of practical knowledge in the workplace. However, universities still struggle to make this crucial linkage due to their reliance on outdated structures and teaching methods. Due to the uncertainty and flux present in the workforce, universities need to provide students with the knowledge-oriented or soft skills that will allow them to transition easily from one job or even field to another. Choise (2016) asserts that in today's society, people make several career changes in their lifetime, perhaps changing their professions up to a total of seven times. In order to succeed in this economic climate, employees need to become what Bountrogianni (2015) refers to as a "specialized generalist" (para. 4), which implies the ability to possess broad skills that transfer easily from one career or industry to another. At the university level, this means that instructors need to train students to not necessarily specialize in a particular field but to acquire abilities that allow them to specialize in a broad range of areas. The authentic learning activities discussed throughout this book will help to provide students with skills that can better adapt their capabilities to the creative economy. The adaptation of universities to the reality of the workforce, however, needs to go beyond individual authentic learning experiences to embrace new learning structures. These structures include a greater focus on cross-curricular programs and courses while eradicating the dependence on the traditional compartmentalization of distinct subject areas. Mintz (2016) discusses the way in which some science programs combine aspects of biology, chemistry, and physics in their courses, while Busl (2015) argues that programs should take a higher-level approach to combine distinct faculties.

In addition to preparing students for the workforce, postsecondary institutions need to support and nurture students towards entrepreneurship. Entrepreneurship constitutes a major aspect of the creative economy, as many small-to-medium enterprises that embrace the creative economy once began as entrepreneurships (World Economic Forum, 2016). As Shepard (2015) reveals, nearly sixty percent of the current generation of students, along with recent graduates, envision themselves as entrepreneurs, suggesting the need for universities to provide students with the appropriate skills and training that will enable them to achieve their goals. Van Wyck (2016) discusses the possibility of entrepreneurship training for students, which involves the provision of mentor and mentee relationships between graduate advisors and students. Additionally, Shepard (2015) suggests the development of networks that link students to entrepreneurs, entrepreneurial coaches, and venture capitalists, thus providing students with the know-how and the funding to start their own ventures. Although entrepreneurship represents a viable alternative for many students, they need to possess the ideal characteristics to succeed in their endeavors, including a desire for freedom and independence, creativity, innovation, job satisfaction, wealth, risk-taking, stamina, devotion, determination, responsibility, and leadership (Alstete, 2008). One of the necessary qualities that defines both entrepreneurship and the creative economy, innovation, can occur radically or incrementally in terms of products, services, processes, business models, or organizational culture (Cram, 2014). In order to prepare students for the innovation required in entrepreneurship, universities can provide students with realistic challenges; for example, three postsecondary institutions in Victoria, BC, Camosun College, University of Victoria, and Royal Roads University, participate in the annual Ready, Set, Solve Challenge, which encourages students to come up with creative solutions for climate change (CRD, 2013). These activities not only constitute prime examples of authentic learning by engaging students with the real world but also provide students with the necessary skills to succeed in the creative economy with entrepreneurship or conventional employment.

The next chapter, Chapter 7, will discuss the benefits of authentic learning within the context of a creative economy. These benefits not only address the academic gains made by students, teachers, and other stakeholders but also examine the way in which authentic learning helps to address the misalignment between universities and the creative economy while filling needed labor gaps in various industries. Rather than focusing on SSA, Chapter 7 provides an international snapshot of how authentic learning will prepare students appropriately for this new, knowledge-based economic modality.

CHAPTER SEVEN
BENEFITS OF AUTHENTIC LEARNING

Authentic Learning is an all Winners Game

FROM STEVE REVINGTON'S MEDIEVAL MARKET TO RABBIT farming in the SSA to climate change challenges in Canadian postsecondary institutions, authentic learning can occur anywhere and anyhow with high-tech or low-tech resources. While implementing authentic learning may seem like an enormous challenge that involves hours upon hours of arduous planning, the benefits that arise from these invaluable activities makes the effort more than worthwhile. Not only does authentic learning increase students' motivation to learn but also provides them with real learning that they can apply in today's creative economy. However, the advantages of this learning style extend far beyond students, reaching teachers, other educators, employers, and even an entire society. Accordingly, this next section of this book will focus on the benefits of authentic learning as classified into two groups: academic benefits and workforce benefits.

ACADEMIC BENEFITS

The academic benefits of authentic learning include increased student motivation, enhanced teacher motivation, improved educational outcomes, and advantages to other stakeholders.

Student Motivation

The literature on authentic learning unanimously demonstrates that this pedagogical method increases the motivation of students to learn. Many of Revington's 12 elements of authentic learning increase student motivation, including role playing, collaboration, and personalized learning (Revington, 2016). Helm (2008) maintains that authentic learning activities engage students of all levels by providing rich, integrated learning experiences. Students who are directly involved in their learning feel excited and curious about their tasks, causing them to delve deeply into their activities (Helm, 2008). Specifically, many of the Canadian education systems have recently proposed changes geared towards the implementation of authentic learning and technology in their individual provinces. For example, the Ontario Public School Boards' Association (2013) has stated that the use of technology in authentic learning increases student motivation by allowing them to pursue individual interests through the multiplicity of available information and resources (OPSBA, 2013). One recent European initiative includes the use of creative classrooms, which constitute innovative learning environments that create realistic opportunities for developing modern labor market skills, such as problem-solving, collaboration, and communication. These classroom environments provide students with the ability to control their own learning through personalized activities that meet their own needs and interests as well as providing leadership opportunities. In this context, teachers serve as guides or mentors that facilitate rather than dictate student learning (Bocconi, Kampylis, & Punie, 2012).

In addition to North American and European examples, research studies from around the world demonstrate similar results about authentic learning, especially in the context of higher learning. In Australia, Faulkner and Faulkner (2012) discuss the motivational effect of several authentic learning opportunities in software engineering programs, which include industry case studies, software tools, and media articles. In Malaysia, Nikitina (2011) provided an example of authentic learning where instructors of foreign languages use theatrical activities, such as the production of drama, videos, or movies for the target language. Not only does this type of activity resemble a real-life context but it also facilitates student enjoyment (Nikitina, 2011). African postsecondary institutions have also shown that authentic learning increases students' desire to learn. Kandiero and Jagero (2014) investigated the effectiveness of Emerging Technologies, a specific authentic learning application, to teach an undergraduate university course in business mathematics at Africa University in Zimbabwe. The authors reported that this application increased the motivation of students to attend class and engage in the material (Kandiero & Jagero, 2014). In addition, a personal interview with a Ugandan university instructor reveals that when he provides enjoyable activities prior to the lecture, students are more likely to participate (M. B. Mulumba, personal communication, April 20, 2017), which further increases the chances of positive learning outcomes. Thus, regardless of the geographical region, the universal appeal of authentic learning is well-demonstrated in both literature and life.

Despite positive findings showing that authentic learning experiences motivate students, Herrington et al. (2004) report that in some cases, teachers who design authentic courses and activities may fail to fully engage some students because authenticity represents a subjective concept based on the teacher's personal perception, thus failing to engage the students' personal backgrounds and interests. The results of this study imply the need for at least some level of student participation in designing or suggesting such activities. Revington (2016) concurs with the need for personalization in his description of the element of personalized experience, which provides students with "personal input" that "allow[s] students to explore their personal interests and creativity," hence providing them with motivation (para. 13). McKenzie, Morgan, Cochrane, Watson, and Roberts (2002) seek to expand the cluster of principles defining authentic learning to enable their students to distinguish genuine authentic learning experiences that speak to their experience in the world. In addition, many students may feel reluctant towards authentic learning because it represents a completely novel approach towards learning. One professor from Uganda's Makerere University recounts his experience upon first introducing authentic learning into his classroom:

> it is not me mainly teaching; they are reading, we are discussing the activities. At first, some students think it is a joke, but eventually they realize there is a lot of learning taking place and they have to really get serious. (C. Mugimu, personal communication, April 28, 2017)

The same professor reports that another motivational issue associated with authentic learning involves the amount of work required; he admits that "students have become increasingly lazy. I find that when request them to do more and read more, they do not want to read. Increasingly, I have noticed students come to class unprepared, which is sometimes frustrating" (C. Mugimu, personal communication, April 28, 2017). Finally, another professor admitted that his use of group work or collaborative learning encouraged student inactivity: "For some students, it even creates laziness, where they do not want to work with others in groups yet they want their names attached to the work" (P. Ssenkusu, personal communication, April 28, 2017). Since authentic learning requires greater levels of student participation, students may feel confused or frustrated that they are being taught in a way that they have never learned, and thus, lack an understanding of what is expected of them. Both literature and personal interviews show that student participation is a necessary component of authentic learning in order to motivate learners. In order to overcome this barrier, students require earlier and heavier exposure to authentic learning, while both students and teachers need to overcome this initial obstacle by persistence rather than simply giving up and reverting to older methods that have already proven to fail.

Teacher Motivation

Not only does authentic learning enhance students' desire to learn, but it also increases the motivation, and hence the performance, of teachers. Although Revington (2016) admits that "this style of learning is labour intensive and time consuming," the enjoyment of planning an exciting learning experience overrides the extra work. In their literature review, Westbrook et al. (2013) found that teachers who implemented interactive learning in their classrooms reported more positive attitudes towards their practice and their students. These authentic learning practices from teachers included continual feedback, linkages between classroom material and student experiences, the establishment of a safe environment, collaborative group activities, the use of authentic materials, student questioning, practical demonstrations, and varying lesson formats. An improvement in teachers' mindsets subsequently influenced students, who experienced improved learning outcomes (Westbrook et al., 2013). Therefore, increased motivation on the part of both teachers and students leads to improved student learning outcomes, discussed further in the next section.

Herrington et al. (2004) investigated the impact of authentic learning activities through web-based courses at the university level. Specifically, these authors found that teachers who design units or courses featuring ongoing authentic learning activities report more enthusiastic and positive attitudes towards their teaching and about the quality of student learning. Specifically, these instructors state that authentic courses and activities enhance their practice by increasing their pedagogical knowledge and personal experience. These results apply to both traditional classroom courses and web-based courses (Herrington et al., 2004). In addition, other studies attest to the way in which authentic learning approaches and tools improve the performance of teachers. Conejar and Kim (2014) found that the use of mobile technologies to deliver authentic learning supports teachers' practice and improves their ability to effectively teach their lessons. Similarly, Banas and York (2014) discovered that the use of authentic learning exercises in pre-service teacher education improved teachers' self-efficacy with technology, which subsequently increased their likelihood to integrate technology in their own practice. In conjunction, these findings demonstrate that teachers require familiarity and understanding with technology prior to implementing these devices as part of authentic learning instructional strategies.

From one perspective, authentic learning can decrease the motivation of teachers to implement this approach, especially given the extensive time commitment. One shortcoming to the use of authentic learning involves the additional time requirements for planning lessons, as many teachers report that they feel taxed with the preparation requirements (Herrington et al., 2004; Revington, 2016). The results of my personal study attested to this issue, as many professors reported that "there is a lot of work to do," which takes away from the valuable time needed to plan authentic learning activities, as teachers "have to be able to prepare for [the] class to ensure authentic learning takes place" (M. B. Mulumba, personal communication, April 20, 2017), thus decreasing instructors' motivation to do so.

This shortcoming may be overcome with additional teacher education on how to effectively incorporate authentic learning in the classroom and actual practice under reasonable time constraints. Revington (2016) extensively discusses the aspect of professional development as part of the authentic learning experience. He states that teachers gain a substantial amount of learning, including new skills, processes, products, services, technologies, knowledge, and network connections. By learning new skills, teachers can subsequently utilize these in subsequent teaching experiences, which enhances teacher motivation.

Teacher Knowledge

In addition to motivating teachers, authentic learning also increases teachers' professional development. Revington (2016) lists professional development as one of his 12 elements of authentic learning. Authentic learning facilitates professional development by allowing teachers to evolve into new roles, learn new teaching methodologies, develop new skills and processes, and enhance their network connections outside of the classroom. While planning an authentic learning opportunity, teachers facilitate student learning rather than feed them content, which allows teachers to learn new delivery approaches. In addition, teachers can learn about different aspects such as products, services, technologies, and processes that occur outside of the classroom and in the real world. Finally, teachers establish new network connections because authentic learning requires them to consult experts, which may include entrepreneurs, employers, corporations, elders, and other professionals in different content areas. Teachers can connect with the community in several ways, including taking students on field trips to visit businesses or sites and inviting guest speakers into the classroom to share their knowledge with students. Other stakeholders, such as parents can serve as valuable resources in facilitating authentic learning opportunities. By engaging in authentic learning, teachers learn a host of valuable skills, methods, and processes that they can subsequently apply to subsequent teaching experiences (Revington, 2016). In sum, the literature demonstrates that authentic learning increases teacher motivation and knowledge, which in turn, also enhances the enjoyment and academic results of students.

Improved Student Outcomes

The final academic benefit of authentic learning involves the ability of this method to improve learning outcomes. According to Helm (2008), authentic learning experiences cause students to increase their engagement with the material, which ultimately influences them to take ownership of their own learning. Specifically, students use critical thinking to develop their own learning strategies and willingly collaborate with other students, two skills strongly associated with authentic learning and the creative economy. When students are motivated to learn material, the amygdala, the part of the brain responsible for emotions and motivation, becomes stimulated, signaling the importance of retaining interesting information (Helm, 2008). Because authentic learning experiences increase students' ability to retain information, these activities and the pedagogical approach that influences such tasks ultimately improves students' academic performance. In addition to the connection between engagement or motivation and learning outcomes, the use of authentic experiences increases the ease of learning through the notion of scaffolding, which involves the connection between new learning material and previous knowledge or experience (Helm, 2008; Orey, 2010). During the process of scaffolding, teachers serve as facilitators that bridge students' previous learning to new information (Orey, 2010).

While studies have shown that traditional teacher-centered methods lead to poor learning outcomes (Otaala et al., 2013), recent research has attested to the practical nature and hence effectiveness of authentic learning. One conventional method of authentic learning involves the use of outdoor education, which incorporates a diverse range of learning experiences that may include outdoor learning activities, tasks conducted outside of the classroom, and education about landscapes and the environment (Higgins & Nicol, 2002). Szczepanski (2006) investigated the effect of outdoor education on students, reporting that this method of authentic learning not only increases student motivation but also enhances educational attainment. Specifically, outdoor learning experiences teach students about the relationship between theory and physical place, thus grounding their education in a real-world context (Higgins & Nicol, 2002). Another type of authentic learning, project-based learning, demonstrates that students engaged in this form of learning outscore students taught by traditional, teacher-centered methods (Bell, 2010)

Despite the efficiency of outdoor learning, authentic learning is delivered most effectively through modern technology. In today's modern society, university courses have begun to incorporate distance or remote education through web-based platforms and resources. Herrington et al. (2004) discusses the implementation of authentic learning through web-based classrooms, showing its effectiveness outside of the traditional classroom. Through establishing a teacher training program in Ethiopia, Zwiers (2007) found that active learning methods such as critical reflection and material that addressed real-world subjects resulted in improved student learning. Furthermore, Campbell (2013) enabled students in a first-year mathematics class to access a database that featured multi-language video explanations of the math concepts. The findings demonstrated that the students with access to the database improved their test scores in comparison to the students that lacked access to the database. Despite the positive effects of using digital technology in the classroom environment, students need to learn digital citizenship in order to obtain skills that appropriately use technology. This includes the development of pro-social skills, education about issues of intellectual property, an understanding of ergonomics, and the avoidance of cyber bullying (OPSBA, 2013). Therefore, the use of modern technology enhances the extent to which authentic learning improves student outcomes.

Other Stakeholders

Authentic learning contains benefits to other stakeholders, including education administrators, policymakers, and governments. In addition to the educational purposes outlined at the outset of the previous chapter, Kampylis and Berki (2014) assert that the main purpose of education should involve preparing students adequately for the future, which includes their contribution to the workforce as well as citizenship responsibilities. With this central purpose in mind, a student's education ultimately affects many stakeholders outside of the education system. Administrators that invest in teacher training programs emphasizing authentic learning reap the benefits of having teachers learn more efficiently and transmitting their knowledge to students through effective learning opportunities (Newmann, King, & Carmichael, 2007). The teacher training programs, and the need for wholesale revisions to such programs in SSA, are discussed in the next chapter. In addition to educational administrators, the national and/or provincial governments that drive policymaking will gain economic advantages by mandating curricular changes that target authentic learning opportunities in the postsecondary classroom. Since the students who engage in authentic learning will possess the necessary skills to succeed in the workforce, the government and education ministers will reap the benefits from academic success as well as a healthy economy.

Unfortunately, my personal interviews with Ugandan university professors reveal the harsh reality that in SSA, many educational administrators perceive the situation in a different way. Some of the instructors revealed that Makerere University intentionally recruits large numbers of students and creates classes of over 1000 students per class in order to maximize profit and minimize costs at the expense of quality. For example, one instructor implied that the university merely focuses on the business aspect, which seeks to procure maximum tuition payments, without worrying about the actual quality of education. He states that the education system "waste[s] time and people's money. The education system does not know how to change, so the entire system is lagging behind" (C. Ssempala, personal communication, April 25, 2017). Another instructor believes that Makerere poorly manages their funds, which leads to the wastage of expenditures that could otherwise be devoted to putting the resources in place that would facilitate authentic learning opportunities (N. Itaaga, personal communication, April 20, 2017). In conjunction, these professors paint a bleak picture of an education system that lacks the willingness to adapt to the modern creative economy for the fear that its immediate profits may be lost. This myopic outlook is harming many students, teachers, and members of the workforce, as discussed in the next section.

ENHANCED PREPARATION FOR WORKFORCE

In addition to its academic benefits, authentic learning also provides advantages to all stakeholders in the workforce: students, employers, and the economy.

Students

Authentic learning contains several benefits for the graduates of postsecondary education. In particular, the authentic learning environment provides students with practical experience that they can apply in the workforce or towards starting their own businesses. McKenzie et al. (2002) perceive authentic learning at the postsecondary level as "a measure of a curriculum's relevance or appropriateness to the world that graduating students will enter" (p. 426). These authors believe that authentic learning not only prepares students for their prospective careers but also readies them for a wide variety of professional and entrepreneurial endeavors. Specifically, authentic learning opportunities at all educational levels enable students to achieve independence and gain important collaboration skills (OPSBA, 2013), two of the skills necessary for the creative economy.

Although education systems should ideally begin authentic learning at early grades, the most crucial level for this type of learning occurs at the postsecondary stage. Instructors who use student-centered learning approaches can enhance the preparation of learners for the workforce by incorporating educational experiences that increase their employability skills, such as creativity, critical thinking, reflection, and problem-solving

(Bunoti, 2010). In a study of Ugandan university instructors, various professors mentioned that authentic learning, as an instructional methodology, encourages critical thinking, creativity, and innovation; as one instructor stated, "The student-centered method really takes innovation and creativity (C. Mugimu, personal communication, April 28, 2017). Creativity and innovation enable students to generate new ideas and refine these ideas into an acceptable format that includes real-world limitations. These skillsets represent essential abilities in a rapidly changing world, thus benefitting students that learn creativity and innovation. Similarly, critical thinking enables students to analyze and understand complex systems representative of today's economy (OPSBA, 2013). Another Makerere professor mentioned the element of collaboration, which, along with networking, allowed his students to thrive (C. Ssempala, personal communication, April 25, 2017). Collaboration within a community of learners, either in a physical or virtual classroom, provides students with the real-world experience of working in teams at their future job setting and dealing with people (Rule, 2006). Due to the phenomenon of globalization, communication and collaboration have gained increasing importance in the modern world, especially with increasing cultural diversity (OPSBA, 2013). Much research has demonstrated the advantages of enabling students to acquire creativity through authentic learning. For instance, Safuan and Soh (2013) investigated the implementation of authentic learning in a Turkish classroom, where the use of Facebook enabled students to develop job-related skills, including analytical thinking, problem solving, and collaboration. Similarly, Neo, Neo, and Tan (2012) reported that the use of technology enhanced student-centered learning and provided students with employable abilities such as creativity and problem solving. In conjunction, these studies show how authentic learning initiatives provide students with real-world skills that will enhance their employability and productivity within the workforce.

Another important area that connects learning to the real world involves the use of technology. Students live in a world where they can access information and communicate with others instantaneously through the use of handheld digital devices. By implementing these devices into the classroom or creating "virtual" classrooms through which students can access material and maintain contact with teachers and peers, educators can enable students to experience a realistic learning environment that not only engages their attention but also bridges the gap between classroom theory and realistic learning experiences (OPSBA, 2013). I Miron, O'Sullivan, and McLoughlin (2000) found that online learning environments for postsecondary students provide realistic settings for students to experience aspects of their desired career while gaining work-related skills. Furthermore, some authors attest to the existence of a relationship between student motivation and employable skills. For example, Hui and Koplin (2011) studied the use of authentic learning in a finance class, where students selected a country to investigate and conducted independent research on this nation. The study results found that students not only experienced engagement in the material but they also acquired the ability to comprehend and solve realistic problems (Hui & Koplin, 2012). Therefore, the use of authentic learning within the postsecondary classroom environment increases the employability of students by providing them with realistic and transferrable skills needed for the creative economy.

Employers

Due to the shifting labor market around the world, employers increasingly require students with specialized and creative skills (Dobbin, 2009; United Nations, 2013). The economies, business sectors, and individual employers in African nations have begun to catch up with the rest of the world in terms of their labor requirements in a service-oriented workforce, which include students with transferrable skills such as creativity, collaboration, reflection, and problem-solving (Barron & Darling-Hammond, 2008). Throughout the world, universities and colleges have the important role of supplying the market with competent graduates that can apply their skills to their new career (Sattler, 2011). Students who graduate from postsecondary institutions with authentic learning environments provide employers with qualified candidates, thus enhancing the strength of their corporations and/or industries. In the modern labor market, employers require that employees possess several employable and transferable skills, which include creativity, problem-solving, flexibility, collaboration, and communication skills (Materu, 2007). Due to the emergence of the creative and knowledge-based labor markets, African economies have undergone recent expansion, requiring increasing numbers of graduates to fulfill labor requirements. In most sectors, skill gaps remain present in these industries, with few graduates qualified for employment (Rwanda Development Board, 2012). In order to fill these skill gaps and provide higher numbers of qualified candidates for all sectors, tertiary learning institutions need to employ authentic learning experiences in their programs.

Researchers have explored the ways in which authentic learning allows students to acquire skills that employers seek. Rule (2006) maintains that authentic learning opportunities that prepare students for the workforce should ultimately impact people outside of the classroom, which can include stakeholders such as employers. In these tasks, students should access resources beyond the immediate learning environment and study real-world problems with relevance to various corporations and industries (Rule, 2006). The results of these activities not only benefit employers by preparing future employees with authentic knowledge and skills but also provide immediate assistance from students' efforts. In particular, work placements such as internships, practicums, and apprenticeships allow students to positively impact an organization with their activities by adding work value and contributing to an organization's mission or culture. Ricardo (2015) maintains that employers interning students gain assistance with special events and short-term projects as well as save costs associated with hiring a part-time or full-time employee in the students' place. In addition, these practical components also benefit workplaces in the same industry or entire industries by providing capable graduates. Some studies have investigated specific ways in which instructors can implement job-based authentic learning in their classroom. For instance, Herrington and Herrington (2006) suggest the idea of web-based learning to mimic the setting of students' prospective work environment by allowing them to solve complex problems. This strategy will increase student preparation in transitioning from the classroom to the workforce, not only benefitting the students but also the employers.

Economy

Finally, the implementation of authentic learning provides substantial benefits to the economy and its various industries. Materu (2007) states that some of the benefits to improving higher education in Africa include technological advancement, improved health, and enhanced quality of life. Some research studies provide concrete evidence that authentic learning achieves these benefits. In fact, a study by Szczepanksi (2006) suggested that outdoor education enhances the health and wellbeing of students. Assuming that the students maintain their level of health into adulthood, the overall wellbeing of people enhances the productivity of workers by minimizing employee absenteeism and turnover as well as increasing performance. From this perspective, a healthier workforce raises not only the performance of individual sectors but also the state of the overall economy. Among all industries in African nations, the healthcare industry will reap substantial benefits, as SSA countries account for twenty-four percent of diseases worldwide yet constitute only four percent of the global workforce (Bingagwaho et al., 2013). Furthermore, the use of technology to deliver authentic learning experiences helps countries to keep up with the pace of technological advancement, which subsequently enhances the economy of various sectors and the overall performance of a nation's economy (OPSBA, 2013). For example, Atkinson (2011) mentions several technological tools that can assist in the implementation of authentic learning: digital stimulation, collaborative wikis, graphing calculators, virtual technology, social media, blogging, discussion forums, and mobile devices. These media and devices not only contribute to the delivery of authentic learning experiences but also educate students in their use, thus enabling these students to contribute their technological knowledge to employers and industries.

Authentic learning initiatives provide direct and indirect benefits to the creative economy. Since authentic learning purports to build certain skills, including creativity and innovation, these skills directly address the abilities sought in the creative economy, which encourages new developments in all fields and industrial sectors. These new innovations ultimately broaden the economy and promote increased specialization in a variety of fields (United Nations, 2013). Because the specialized, service-based economy already requires critical thinking and problem-solving skills best addressed by authentic learning opportunities (Dobbin, 2009), the forecasted trend towards greater innovation and specialization to meet rapid change makes authentic learning even more critical within the emerging creative economy. In addition, authentic learning tasks that target cultural and linguistic aspects not only teach students about foreign languages in realistic ways but also enhance their sense of international diversity and multiculturalism necessary in today's global economy (Alidou et al., 2006; Nikitina, 2011). The development of culture and language provides students with the necessary tools for participating in the creative economy not only in their own nations but also internationally. Furthermore, the objectives of authentic learning align with those of creative economy initiatives. As previously mentioned, authentic learning, as well as the general methodology of constructivism, empowers individual learners by focusing on their strengths, weaknesses, needs, and interests (Radu 2011; Westbrook, 1993). Similarly, the creative economy aims to empower citizens by focusing on their culture; specifically, "it empowers people with capacities to take ownership of their own development process" (United Nations, 2013, p. 9). By encouraging multiple perspectives and embracing collaboration, the creative economy reflects the goals of authentic learning. Therefore, authentic learning represents the ideal educational approach for sustaining the creative economy.

In addition to the economy, authentic learning can enable students to manage their general affairs in life as well as maintain a reasonable level of civic participation. Authentic learning can teach adults to function effectively in society through various tasks: balancing a budget, making an informed decision on a political candidate, choosing a major purchase such as a home or car, planning for a family, negotiating with salespeople, and persuading an organization to change its policies (Newmann et al., 2007). Interestingly, these practical tasks recall the purposes of Indigenous African Education, where Indigenous African children learned how to perform tasks necessary for survival. The successful execution of such duties requires the skills developed through authentic learning opportunities, such as critical thinking, decision-making, collaboration, communication, and innovation. For example, the authentic learning skill of collaboration, executed through involvement in cooperative learning within a community of learners, prepares students for dealing with people in various facets of life (Rule, 2006). As a result, students should receive similar tasks in the academic learning environment in order to not only mirror these real-world activities but also to hone the crucial skills required to perform their civic duties and function in society (Newmann et al., 2007). Some of these tasks can include the use of bus schedules, maps, diaries, and interviews as a way of developing critical literacy (Rule, 2006). Although the aspect of day-to-day activities seems to have little relationship to the economy, these daily activities ultimately impact the economy through financial elements such as purchasing, budgeting, and bill paying. From this perspective, authentic learning in education ultimately impacts the economy not only directly, as discussed in the preceding section, but also indirectly, through a person's ability to perform basic life activities. While this chapter showed the benefits of authentic learning, the final chapter of this book, Chapter 8, discusses the barriers and opportunities for implementing authentic learning in SSA.

CHAPTER EIGHT
IMPLEMENTING AUTHENTIC LEARNING IN SSA

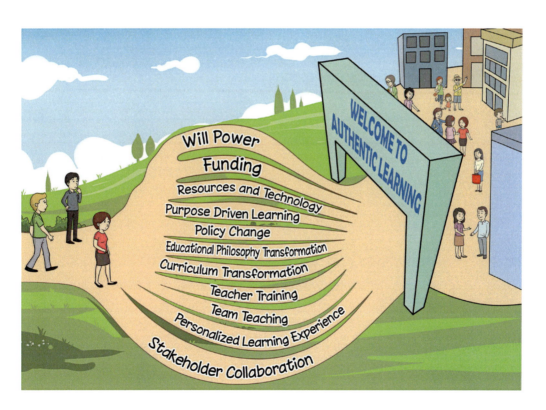

The Road to Implementing Authentic Learning

NOW THAT WE HAVE LEARNED ABOUT THE IMPORTANCE of authentic learning in preparing students for the creative economy, the final chapter of this book will discuss the proposed changes that can enable African nations to implement authentic learning at the postsecondary level. Although the following sections provide subdivisions between the various areas of potential improvement, keep in mind that each part works interdependently with the other parts, thus working symbiotically together as a single organism as envisioned by Sir Ken Robinson. However, the use of subsections provides an organized and systematic way for the reader to understand the several areas as separate issues that require improvement.

FUNDING

Most African nations and their various industries face challenges in terms of their human and financial capital. Many national and international organizations have significantly increased their funding for education in African countries (Watkins, 2013). However, a report by the Education for All (EFA) (2014) initiative indicates that the world's richest nations possess the resources to contribute even greater amounts to this cause. The same report also maintains that the establishment of specific target objectives, such as six to seven percent from national governments and twenty percent from international donors, will ensure that the money devoted towards African education receives proper utilization (EFA, 2014). Some of the potential new uses for funding include the establishment of quality assurance programs to oversee education and greater teacher training (Materu, 2007) as well as the development of local research initiatives that encourage the acquisition of local knowledge and innovation (Teferra & Greijn, 2010). Specifically, the development of new knowledge may bolster the creative economy by providing businesses and graduates with unique and culturally-relevant innovations (United Nations, 2013). In addition, new potential donors, such as national governments and local business, can emerge as major contributors to this effort (Watkins, 2013). The contributions from businesses and corporations will enhance the link between education and the workforce, thus providing a greater sense of stakeholder accountability from businesses seeking new graduates. Although these sources propose several ways of raising money, such as additional donations, increased taxation, and reallocation of taxpayer funds as well as the suggested uses for such funds, such literature fails to specify the ways to ensure the planned utilization of such funds.

While international donors have focused their funding mainly on basic education, such as literacy and numeracy in the primary grades, tertiary education has received the least amount of attention in these countries. In addition, some of the funding devoted towards international education has been allocated to postsecondary education in developing countries such as China, largely neglecting the needs of underdeveloped nations (EFA, 2014). Bloom et al. (2006) state that African nations, especially Sub-Saharan Africa, have the lowest enrollment rates in the world. While the enrollment rates in African postsecondary institutions have doubled in the past decade, the higher number of students has resulted in a low quality of education in these institutions (British Council, 2014), thus necessitating the input of more money to improve the quality of education. It is not only external funding from national and international bodies that represent a major concern, however. Interviews with instructors from Makerere University reveal that issues surrounding internal funding represent a significant obstacle in their teaching experience. One professor reveals that, in fact, the university's administration possesses adequate funds, but they suffer from poor asset management (N. Itaaga, personal communication, April 20, 2017). Thus, not only do African universities lack financial support, but the universities that do possess adequate funds, such as Makerere, tend to manage these funds improperly.

The acquisition of additional funding for higher education will enable African universities to adequately address increasing enrollment rates and provide a higher quality of education to growing numbers of students. Future speculations show that additional investments in higher education will lead to a GDP growth rate of at least 0.24 percent, which more than recovers the costs of the initial investment (Bloom et al., 2006). Ssentamu (2013) suggests some funding initiatives that may increase the financial support towards higher education in Africa. Specifically, he suggests the addition of publicly funded postsecondary institutions, the implementation of a student loan scheme, the creation of partnerships that enhance the potential for networking between sponsoring agencies and universities, and the involvement of private sector corporations in higher education (Ssentamu, 2013). As previously indicated, the role of corporations in funding postsecondary education will enhance the connection between education and business while potentially influencing other important changes, such as curricular revisions that directly address modern workforce needs. Additional funding initiatives will enhance authentic learning opportunities by not only raising the quality of education but also providing additional resources and technology to facilitate such a wholesale change.

RESOURCES AND TECHNOLOGY

One of the main barriers for implementing authentic learning in African countries concerns the dearth of material and technological resources. Since most authentic learning initiatives involve the use of modern technology (Herrington, 2009; Herrington & Herrington, 2007; Lombardi, 2007; Oblinger, 2007; Parker et al., 2013), SSA nations, which lack the technological capital of wealthier nations, are at a significant disadvantage for implementing authentic learning. However, some studies, cited mainly in Chapter 5, have indicated ways in which teachers can implement authentic learning despite limited resources. In his study, Zwiers (2007) found that instructors have the potential to implement active learning methods without utilizing elaborate resources or modern technology. Some of these approaches include reflection, problem solving, creativity, open-ended questioning, and critical thinking. Some Makerere university professors have described various creative initiatives that they implemented, including the use of collaborative learning, problem-solving challenges, and class discussions, which involve minimal technological investments. In addition, authentic learning can occur during outdoor-based education or field trips as mentioned throughout Chapter 5 (Hein, 1999; Higgins & Nicol, 2002; Moos & Honkomp, 2014; Szczepanski, 2006). Finally, Alidou et al. (2006) suggest that teachers can provide interactive learning experiences through access to local animals. In conjunction, these studies suggest that teachers can utilize authentic learning experiences despite limited resources.

Furthermore, other research has suggested methods for inexpensively implementing enhanced technological resources in African universities. Herrington and Herrington (2007) assert that the use of modern technology in universities and colleges enhances instructors' capacity to provide authentic learning experiences, while Ssentamu (2013) maintains that teachers can incorporate technology to effectively manage large classes or lectures and increase the educational opportunities for poorer or rural students. Consequently, teachers need to learn how to deliver lessons using such devices. A report by Simpson (2013) proposed the implementation of interactive radio and television to reach students that lack access to traditional education settings and systems, thus providing increased access to disadvantaged, special needs, and geographically isolated students. Among fifteen international case studies on this educational use of technology, South Sudan implemented an interactive radio instruction project that involved nearly 500,000 students from 2006 to 2011. These pupils received thirty-minute lessons in English, the local language, math, and life skills. Due to the live broadcasting of these programs, they serve as a platform for discussion, hence attesting to their interactive nature. The findings of these studies showed the potential for such technologies to improve learning outcomes and overcome educational barriers such as geographical access, poor infrastructure, political conflict, and teacher qualification (Simpson, 2013)

Another potential form of modern tools that SSA can implement into education involves mobile technology. In their pilot study, Traxler and Dearden (2005) investigated the use of SMS mobile technology in teacher education by establishing a distance-based learning program that delivered education to students despite the remoteness of their location. Specifically, the authors examine wholesale efforts to implement the widespread use of this technology in Kenya with the collaboration of policymakers, IT personnel, and educators (Traxler & Dearden, 2005). This study raises some promising opportunities, especially due to its cost-effectiveness; ability to connect the various stakeholders in postsecondary education; and its provision of several resources, including content, conferences, links, reminders, resources, and asynchronous conversations. More recently, Swaffield, Jull, and Ampah-Mensah (2013) discuss the use of Skype, a video and voice messaging service in Ghana as "a cost-effective solution that offered the functionality… to send out and receive messages to large numbers of recipients efficiently" (p. 1297). Despite the potential effectiveness of SMS technology, this research overlooks issues concerning the accessibility of SMS in remote areas of Kenya and other SSA nations. Poor cellular access in rural areas requires expensive data plans, which many students and families in SSA may lack the ability to afford, compromising the effectiveness of this project. Future studies may investigate the implementation of community WiFi hotspots in schools as a means of overcoming this barrier.

Other research argues that the implementation of modern technology increases access to quality learning opportunities. Conejar and Kim (2014) assert that the use of mobile devices, including phones, tablets, e-readers, apps, and online learning platforms, can enhance the access, equity, and quality of education. Although these devices seem expensive, the cost of new technology has dropped substantially, perhaps eventually making them affordable even in developing countries. In addition, the expenses of purchasing these devices offsets other expenditures, including books, learning materials, and transportation (Conejar & Kim, 2014; Ssentamu, 2013). Despite infrastructural barriers, a few professors at Makerere University, as discussed in earlier sections of the book, have implemented technology, including an online learning platform and Google Docs. The cost of technology can undergo further reduction through the free and open access of online educational resources, which makes education more affordable and accessible around the world (European Commission, 2014; Hogan et al., 2015). Thus, despite the limited resources present in African countries, these nations can implement authentic learning experiences with or without modern technology.

POLICY

In the minds of many educators, the first requirement for implementing authentic learning into postsecondary classrooms starts with governmental policy, which ultimately controls the development of curricula. Specifically, African governments need to develop mandatory policies for the inclusion of authentic learning opportunities in the curriculum and centralized approaches for monitoring and evaluating these policies. Jaffer et al. (2007) mention that although most African nations have the impetus to reform educational policy to reflect workforce requirements, the progress has been stalled due to political issues in some countries, such as the Rwandan genocide of 1993 (Republic of Rwanda, 2003). In addition, the governments or policymakers may lack the knowledge of how to change; a participant in my study of Makerere University professors revealed that Makerere lags behind in its approach to teaching and the administration resists change (C. Ssempala, personal communication, April 25, 2017). Several authors have made various suggestions for policy improvement, including the use of divisions and subdivisions that reflect the levels of education and the curricular subject areas (Republic of Rwanda, 2003) as well as changes that permit multilingual education, allowing instruction in both local and dominant foreign languages (Alidou et al., 2006). The policies surrounding higher learning institutions also require revision. One of the challenges associated with postsecondary education involves poor governance (Materu, 2007). In addition, Jumani and Jumani (2013) reported that the process of curricular reformation contains several obstacles, such as a lack of agreement among policymakers and other stakeholders. These challenges affect other areas of education, including teacher training and recruitment, which currently suffers from a lack of centralized governance in pre-service and in-service training (University of London, 2010).

Moreover, Teferra and Greijn (2010) suggest that African governments need to make policy changes that aim at enhancing the existence of local knowledge and innovation. This modification would reduce the reliance on imported information and research, providing universities and industries with more local knowledge and talent. The recent emergence of the creative economy has stimulated growth in many countries worldwide. One of the Makerere University instructors suggests that professors looking to retool their pedagogical approaches should study or attend conferences abroad in order to learn about the student-centered methods taught in North American and European schools (C. Mugimu, personal communication, April 28, 2017). Although the acquisition of international knowledge will help SSA countries to learn new teaching methods, these nations still have the need to develop a broader home-grown knowledge base that better connects graduates with the economy. Some solutions for amending this problem involve greater collaboration amongst and within various industrial sectors, which not only generates new knowledge but also creates jobs and overcomes skills gaps in existing industries (United Nations, 2013). Kampylis and Berki (2014) discuss the emergence of successful start-up businesses in Africa. While some case studies exist to support local knowledge and innovation, the relative novelty of this aspiration requires further investigation.

Apart from the development of policy, another challenge in the area of policy involves implementation. According to educator Sir Ken Robinson, many policymakers lack the motivation or mindset for change. In his video "How to change education," Robinson suggests that government and policymakers adapt to the need for change and increase their awareness of the smaller scale developments that are occurring in education, such as Massive Open Online Courses (MOOCs) and the use of technology in the classrooms. By recognizing their integral role in the system, governments will ideally realize that the excessive focus on standards harms rather than helps the education system and make changes accordingly (Robinson, 2013). This static mindset is reflected in my personal conversations with Ugandan professors teaching at Makerere University, most of whom concur that government administration, educational managers, and educational policymakers provide negligible support to teachers. Moreover, while a significant amount of funds has been devoted towards policy development, these plans often fail to reach the implementation stage due to a lack of knowledge and direction for implementing the policies. A paucity of literature currently discusses ways in which stakeholders such as policymakers, education administrators, and teachers can collaborate effectively to implement existing policies for authentic learning initiatives in SSA higher education. Future studies can investigate effective ways for these stakeholders to cooperatively establish and follow policy directions.

EDUCATIONAL PHILOSOPHY

As mentioned at the outset of the book, educational philosophies have transitioned from Indigenous learning, to teacher-centered learning, and, only now, are beginning to make strides towards student-centered learning. While western educational philosophies recognize the importance of authentic learning, SSA countries still continue to use teacher-centered instructional pedagogies in Africa. The cultural ideologies in Africa emphasize collectivism rather than individualism, which influences Africans to conceive the importance of individuals in terms of their contribution to a given group or society. This perspective results in the belief that all students possess the same learning abilities and the delivery of a one-size-fits-all education (Vavrus et al., 2011). In addition, this belief causes Africans to perceive the purpose of education as preparing students for their role in a larger community or society, where collective values take priority over individual needs and interests. Furthermore, in African countries, the cultural perception of education views the teacher as a central authority figure requiring respect from the students. Specifically, students conceive the teacher as an objective and distant dictator that disseminates knowledge rather than a guide or mentor that facilitates student learning (King, 2011). This attitude leads to the corporal punishment that occurred when I was a student and still occurs today with my daughter's friends in Ugandan primary schools.

This central tenet of collectivism and social hierarchy causes philosophical complications in implementing student-centered approaches, which provide students with control over their own learning (Paludan, 2006). Based on the stark disparities between the educational philosophies of SSA and those of the western world, the problem of overcoming inertia or resistance to change and embracing change represents a possible obstacle to implementing modifications in educational philosophies throughout SSA nations. My doctoral study that investigated the attitudes of Ugandan professors revealed that the administration of many universities still holds elitist and outdated beliefs, which cause them to resist change. One particular professor explained:

> There are definite problems at the top. They still believe that Makerere instructors should just lecture and pass students through the system. The school is too expensive; it is all about making money. Nobody from the ministry cares about the quality of education; nobody bothers about value addition. They are still stuck in the old ideals that to get into Makerere enhances status and reputation. (C. Ssempala, personal communication, April 25, 2017)

The notion of "passing students through the system" strongly echoes the words of Ken Robinson and Prince EA, both of whom envision today's education system as a type of assembly line, as well as my own personal experience in which students passed from grade to grade without anyone knowing whether they had mastered the abilities required at the previous levels of education. Bar-Yam, Rhoades, Sweeney, Kaput, and Bar-Yam (2002) discuss how educational changes must involve wholesale systematic changes rather than isolated and fragmented modifications to various parts of the system. In order to achieve this goal, we must somehow convince the people at the top that they need to consider moving forward with major revisions, which include the implementation of authentic learning.

As mentioned, African nations suffer from a lack of original ideas and materials, requiring them to import knowledge and resources from other countries, such as those in Europe and North America (Teferra & Greijn, 2010). This cultural importation perpetuates the existence of traditional pedagogical approaches because teachers lack mastery over foreign knowledge and languages, thus causing them to revert to fact-based approaches to instruction, such as rote learning and simple recall. Similarly, African nations contain extreme cultural, ethnic, religious, and linguistic diversity among the students, which ultimately hinders the development of novel pedagogical approaches (Rudman, 2013). Another issue stalling the implementation of learner-centered educational philosophies involves the concept of educational inertia, which maintains that individuals and systems experience difficulty in overcoming the rigid nature of established values or systems (Paludan, 2006). Part of the problem relating to inertia involves the age-old belief that associates a university degree with elitism. Both research (European Commission, 2014) and personal interviews pointed to the reality that in some parts of the world, a sense of elitism still exists within the university administration, which causes these universities to persist in teacher-centered methods that reject vocational training (N. Itaaga, personal communication, April 20, 2017). Due to the persistence of traditional educational philosophies, students and teachers may require a significant period of adjustment (Vavrus et al., 2011), which a few of the Makerere University professors attempting to implement student-centered learning approaches have already experienced. Many students accustomed to conventional teacher-centered methods may experience an initial period of frustration and resistance with lengthy projects that appear to lack a place in traditional education (Herrington et al., 2004; Oblinger, 2007). By changing the purpose of education to reflect its importance in preparing students for the workforce and realizing the demands of the new creative and knowledge-based economy, governments and educators can realize the crucial nature of placing authentic learning in the curriculum.

CURRICULUM

The curricula in African postsecondary institutions require updating in order to enable authentic learning in the university classroom. Specifically, the literature demonstrates consensus in its assertion that most or all university and college programs should include practical components, such as field placements, practicums, clinical practice, internships, and apprenticeships (Resnick, 1987). The implementation of field placements and practical internships in SSA postsecondary education poses several barriers, including the skills gap in the existing workforce, the paucity of funds, and the inadequate infrastructure in many countries (Rwanda Development Board, 2012; Traxler & Dearden, 2005). In fact, one professor in my research study seemed to indicate that despite the attempt to provide students at Makerere with internships, there were not enough placements (N. Itaaga, personal communication, April 20, 2017). The inclusion of such practical components can overcome resource limitations by requiring students to complete work experience segments as part of the mandatory curriculum without compensation. In addition, the presence of students in industry will assist in filling the skills gap, as students possess at least a basic grasp of the theoretical understanding required in their desired field. The collaboration among students and working professionals can enhance the knowledge and skills of both parties; the professionals can share their hands-on experience with students while the students can supplement the professionals' experience with increased theoretical information. Since this teaching and learning exchange will occur on the job, the economy will retain and increase its current workforce capital without incurring additional expenditures. Thus, the addition of practical components in postsecondary courses will address existing skills gaps in several major sectors, including construction, health, and agriculture (Republic of Rwanda Ministry of Health, 2013; Rwanda Development Board, 2012).

In addition, program designs need to establish a clear link between the theoretical classroom material and the practical experience in order to provide students with transferrable skills that will enable them to obtain employment upon graduation. One of my colleagues mentioned her frustration with the apparent disconnect between theory and practice in her teacher education program, which made the theory seem meaningless, as the college emphasized that employers only looked at a student's practicum results. One way in which the curriculum can reflect more authentic learning experiences involves a greater integration among subject areas (McKenzie et al., 2002). Specifically, some researchers suggest that university curricula incorporate multidisciplinary and interdisciplinary programs with courses from a variety of traditional subject areas (Jaffer et al., 2007; Teferra & Greijn, 2010). This modification would provide a more realistic means of delivering subject material, as, in the real world, jobs and professions integrate knowledge from various fields or disciplines. Another area of possible improvement involves a redesigning of the current curriculum to emphasize vertical rather than horizontal learning. With the current curricular structure, teachers feel compelled to address all of the information in the curriculum, influencing them to "teach to the test." In this format, education focuses on the shallow and fragmented exploration of many disparate areas rather than deep exploration of major ideas (McTighe, Seif, & Wiggins, 2004). To address this issue, Teferra and Greijn (2010) propose that the government emphasize fewer disciplines or major curricular areas focused on a broad national knowledge base. Thus, a reformatting of the curriculum will help to facilitate authentic learning at the postsecondary level.

Researchers provide several specific examples of current initiatives from programs that connect theory to practice. For instance, a British study proposed scenario-based classroom learning as a means of bridging theoretical classroom material with professional placement programs (Errington, 2011). Another study examined a methodology termed service learning, where students explore community issues as part of their classroom curriculum (Mariappan, Monemi, & Fan, 2005). In an Australian university setting, Stein, Isaacs, and Andrews (2004) investigate a business management course in which an instructor used authentic learning to connect the artificial classroom environment with the realistic work environment. Focusing explicitly on African countries, Zwiers (2007) suggested that curricular revisions aimed at incorporating active learning experiences could require students to develop active participation in relevant community issues, examine the history and culture of a given community or society, hone communication skills in a realistic manner, and establish positive personality traits. Curricular guidelines should also focus on the teaching of transferrable "soft" skills, such as collaboration, problem-solving, interpersonal relationships, communication, critical thinking, innovation, and leadership (British Council, 2014). Postsecondary institutions also need to teach students about the effective use of contemporary information and communication technology and the ways in which to apply this technology for enhancing their employability (Teferra & Greijn, 2010). In addition to employing the work placement component, African universities can learn from these models and use similar initiatives to transform the classroom into a more authentic learning environment that involves real-world situations.

In addition, educational systems in the 21st Century should be aligned with structural transformations that are happening globally. Educators, parents, governments and other education stakeholders, should start probing the education system and ask the hard question: Are we training our children and equipping then with necessary skills that can be sustainable in the 21st century? Even though many growth and development economists seemed to have believed that globalization and its associated outcomes would make rapid structural transformation inescapable, experiences from most of Sub-Saharan Africa in general and Uganda in particular have so far proved otherwise. It is quite astonishing that the overall trajectory of de-industrialization policies of the 1970s and 80s continues to dominate. As the chart (in Figure 1) below illustrates, Ugandan workforce have been stuck in the primitive rudimentary agricultural systems with almost no vertical mobility to the new industries and services. Part of this slow structural transformation of African workers to industry can be explained by educational systems whose curriculum no longer prepares students to take advantage of the ever-evolving technological advancement. What is more disturbing in contemporary times is that the speed by which automation is displacing workers is inconceivable. It is already happening globally, and it will get worse in developing countries if the educational curriculum is not overhauled (Ojede, 2018).

Figure 1: Uganda's Employment Shares in Agriculture, Industry and Services

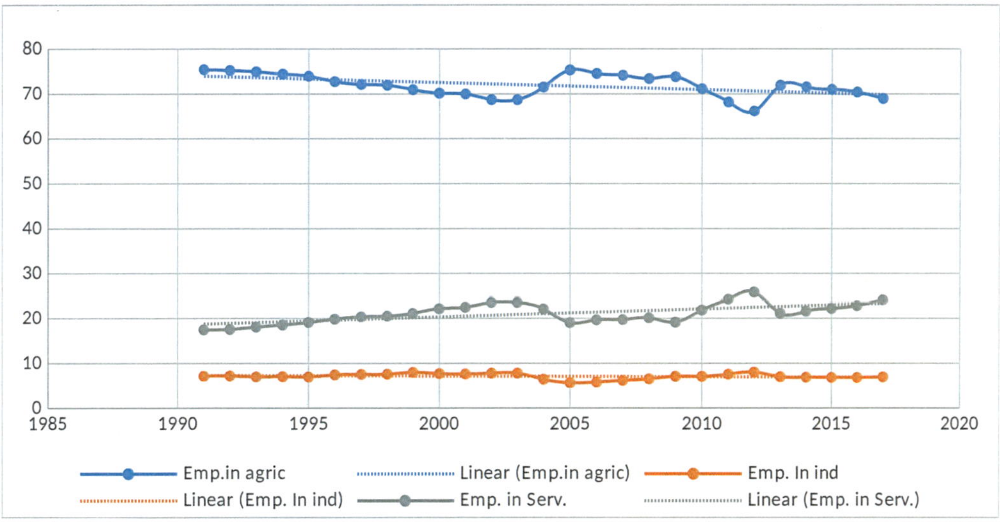

Data Source: The World Bank World Development Indicators and the United Nations-International Labor Organization

TEACHER TRAINING

In his video "How to change education" (2013), Sir Ken Robinson argues that the entire teaching and learning relationship constitutes the crux of education. The educational revolution that he proposes involves reconfiguring this teaching and learning process by starting with the premise that children already have the desires and mechanisms to acquire knowledge. Unfortunately, the current education system, which exposes children to buildings, classrooms, and grades, kills that desire to learn. Rather than force-feeding students mass clusters of information that may or may not interest them, teachers need to step out of their role, largely forced on them by the education system, as knowledge couriers, and embrace teaching as a type of art form in which to excite, engage, and motivate students to learn (Robinson, 2013). In fact, Robinson concurs with Revington's concept of the facilitator, whereby teachers encourage students to actively teach themselves. Thus, teachers need to change their mindset and incorporate the authentic learning techniques discussed in Chapter 3 of this book. Unlike other educators, who take a top-down approach and point at the administration or policymakers as the prime mover behind the education system, Robinson asserts that a bottom-up approach is required in education. Based on the conception of education as a live organism with interdependent parts, he proposes that teachers themselves can change the system by changing the aspects of education that they can control, including their practice and their classroom environment. With one teacher changing their ways, Robinson suggests that other teachers will eventually follow in the footsteps of the first teacher, and policymakers may even eventually take note, forcing them to make changes (Robinson, 2013). This sentiment was echoed in my interviews with Ugandan professors, one of whom stated that when a few teachers implemented authentic learning in his institution, other teachers were intrigued by the new method:

> When we started this new method, everybody was interested. Some people asked us how we do it. Others came in and sat to watch our teaching. In the beginning, we experienced challenges because many of the stakeholders presented reasons that it will not work. The process of co-organizing something new is not easy, but we stuck to our guns. However, some people immediately adopted our methods; there is a lady here, and there are so many others. (C. Ssempala, personal communication, April 25, 2017)

This testament supports Robinson's notion of education as an organic concept whose parts interact symbiotically rather than linearly as a top-down hierarchy. Although a single teacher or even small group of teachers may have limited power within the larger system, their actions can slowly set in motion changes that can perhaps reach the top.

In addition to training teachers in authentic learning methods, teacher training in SSA can also strive to improve the quality of teachers. The shortage and low quality of teachers in African university settings demonstrates the need for improved teacher training and recruitment programs (Bunoti, 2010). Many potential teachers and instructors feel reluctant to enter the profession because of poor working conditions, including high student-teacher ratios, the presence of disease and poverty, poor infrastructural environments, and low pay (World Bank, 2011). When supplied with adequate resources, governments need to increase instructor pay to meet basic living standards or provide them with additional benefits, such as subsidized housing as well as non-monetary benefits like awards and promotion opportunities (EFA 2014; World Bank, 2011). The existence of poor teachers using outdated teaching methods merely perpetuates problems with teacher training. Otaala Maani, and Bakaira (2013) found that most teachers attribute their pedagogical approaches to their teacher education and standardized national exams. These results suggest that teacher training, curriculum designs, and examination content should undergo revision as a means of moving away from teacher-centered learning.

One of the first changes required to address such deficiencies involves centralized governance, which leads to standardization of knowledge, authentic pedagogical approaches, and legitimate instructor credentials (University of London, 2010). Current teacher training colleges lack government regulations and oversight, resulting in a lack of accountability (Vavrus et al., 2011). Moreover, traditional teacher education programs in African countries use the technical rationality model, which teaches technical skills to deliver instruction, rather than the reflective practitioner model, which prompts teachers to develop their own pedagogical style on the basis of previous and emerging instructional models (Otaala et al., 2013; Vavrus et al., 2011). A Ugandan professor provided a similar observation using different terminology; when describing the evolution of teacher training methods at Makerere, he stated that the university "started with The Craft Model, but currently, we are following what we call The Applied Sciences Model, where we first bring students into the university, teach them for some time, and give them content" (M. B. Muluma, personal communication, April 20, 2017). The applied science model, like the technical rationality model, focuses on theory, content, and isolated skill development, while the craft or reflective practitioner model concentrates more strongly on the practicums by putting education students in the real environment and teaching them critical thinking skills. This reliance on conventional ways of instructing new teachers results in the development of teacher-centered pedagogies. In addition to outdated models of teacher training, issues such as language barriers (Alidou et al., 2006), limited resources, and poor infrastructure (Traxler & Dearden, 2005) also undermine the quality of teacher education in African universities.

Despite the reliance on traditional teacher instruction models, teacher training methods have shown some recent improvement, leading to the promotion of a learner-centered approach in SSA countries. Many teachers feel challenged by their lack of familiarity with the foreign language in which they must teach, leading them to use teacher-centered instructional approaches such as chorus, repetition, recall, and memorization (Alidou et al., 2006). Language barriers result from the regional mobility of teachers and the mandated policy to instruct in a second language, such as English, French, or Spanish (Alidou et al., 2006; Zwiers, 2007). Another aspect of teacher training that demonstrates gaps involves the use of technology. Banas and York (2014) reported that while many teachers express comfort with using technology in lesson planning and communication, they lack the ability or desire to integrate it in their lesson delivery. These authors subsequently indicated that teachers who have experience and understanding with using technology to provide lesson material demonstrate a greater likelihood of using technology in content delivery (Banas & York, 2014). Similarly, Rule (2006) asserts that pre-service teachers require meaningful opportunities to apply authentic learning in classroom exercises and practicum placements.

Once pre-service teachers have received their education and training in school practice, many teachers lack a proper orientation to the expectations and methods of their respective schools. Personal experiences and interviews with instructors at Uganda's Makerere University reveal the dire need to better orient teachers into their new roles. As an economics major hired to teach both privately and in a class setting, I had not received any formal orientation from my employers. The stories of Makerere professors mirror the experiences that I had, as nearly all professors interviewed in my doctoral study echo the need for better orientation into their institutions. The majority of professors concurred that they were merely handed a syllabus and shown the classroom in which they must teach. One instructor explained that the head of his department

> pointed out where the classroom was and told me that the students attend lectures from there. If you are lucky, he will come and introduce you to the class. If you are not, they will just tell you to go to G1, which is where the students attend the lectures, and that your class runs from 8 am to 10 am on Monday. Nobody will transition you into that. (N. Itaaga, personal communication, April 20, 2017)

The lack of transition or orientation that professors receive into their institution's expected methods and policies represents yet another startling deficiency in teacher training. Not surprisingly, most of the professors interviewed in the study maintained that Makerere, as well as other universities in Uganda and throughout SSA, needs to implement a program or process for orienting new teachers into the institution. The suggestions for such a program included a series of workshops or seminars, an ongoing mentorship with senior or associate professors, greater administrative support services for new instructors, study abroad programs that allow teachers to learn methods from other countries, and formal training on appropriate methodologies.

With regards to training on methodologies, in-service teachers can also make adaptations to their practices by learning how to engage in curriculum planning for authentic learning (Jumani & Jumani, 2013). Kangai and Bukaliya (2011) suggest the use of distance education as a means of increasing the opportunities for aspiring as well as current teachers to obtain the necessary credentials, thus increasing the number of qualified teachers. African nations can also improve the ongoing professional development opportunities available to in-service teachers. The literature recommends initiatives such as teacher workshops or forums; professional learning communities; teacher collaboration with administrators, faculty/staff of higher education institutions, and businesses; mentoring or support from peers and supervisors; peer assessment, and online distance learning initiatives (Kanuka & Nocente, 2002; Potts & Schlichting, 2011; Reitsma & van Hamburg; 2013; Westbrook et al., 2013). The research has suggested that some of these improvements to teacher training programs may improve the knowledge, quality, performance, and pedagogical methods of teachers, eradicating problems associated with unqualified university instructors (Bunoti, 2010; EFA, 2014) and establishing more authentic learning opportunities that connect education directly to modern workforce requirements. King (2011) discusses Ethiopia's Higher Diploma Programme, a mandatory teacher education program, which implements five components associated with student-centered pedagogies, such as active learning, ongoing assessment, reflective exercises, major research projects, and a work placement. Other African countries can utilize similar examples to provide teachers with quality education geared towards authentic learning.

One possible obstacle to the use of in-service training for working teachers involves the existing teacher shortage in SSA countries, as discussed at length in Chapter 4. Since these countries have an insufficient number of qualified teachers, these nations possess even fewer capable substitute teachers. Despite this teacher shortage, SSA countries can still implement successful professional development programs by enabling working teachers to complete the workshops and courses during their personal downtime, such as evenings, weekends, holidays, and summer breaks. Some of the professors at Makerere University emphasized their hectic schedule, which involves research, marking, committee participation, graduate student supervision, and school practice involvement on top of teaching (S. W. Wafula, personal communication, April 20, 2017). Although teachers may feel overwhelmed by the additional commitment, these courses can provide incentives, such as increased pay and funded travel (EFA, 2014; World Bank, 2011). In addition, many of these courses can be delivered in an online and interactive manner, which saves travelling funds and the need for substitute teachers while overcoming obstacles associated with inadequate infrastructure (Diamond & Gonzalez, 2014; Kangai & Bukaliya, 2011; Kanuka & Nocente, 2012; Traxler & Dearden, 2005).

STAKEHOLDER COLLABORATION

The final area that requires consideration entails the collaboration amongst multiple stakeholders, including governments, institutions, program designers, instructors, and students. Ken Robinson maintains that the major problem in connecting stakeholders originates from the way in which educators envision the school system; for centuries, the education system has adopted a mechanical rather than an organic metaphor, treating students as homogenized group and feeding them a mass-produced or "fast food" type of education while plodding them through the system as cattle (Robinson, 2013). Rather, Robinson asserts that educators should conceptualize the education system as an organic entity with interrelated and interdependent parts that are in constant flux and that adapt to their environment.

Most African nations feature weak links between the various stakeholders, resulting in any authentic learning initiatives to appear fragmented and ineffective on a broad scale. These weak links result in ambiguity concerning the mission of education as well as lack of student engagement and the perpetuation of teacher-centered approaches (Newmann et al., 2007). The dearth of qualified teachers, government officials and education administrators, who lack the training and knowledge required to monitor and evaluate educational outcomes, results in other problems, such as apathy from parents and ministers (Watkins, 2013). Unfortunately, as my interviews with Ugandan professors revealed, significant gaps exist between the expectations of university administrators and the realistic needs of instructors. Specifically, university administrators merely assume that most professors have received the proper training in education without realizing the existence of skills gaps; "the assumption is that they are recruiting people who have done education and are already teachers, so they know already what to do" (P. Ssenkusu, personal communication, April 20, 2017). However, this assumption, as discussed in the previous section, is generally erroneous, leading to untrained instructors struggling to teach their classes and resulting in poor learning outcomes. These detrimental outcomes point to the necessity for improved collaboration amongst all stakeholders in education, including those involved in the transition period from graduation to workforce participation.

Wholesale changes that motivate a shift from the traditional teacher-centered mode of instruction to student-centered education require the involvement and coordination of all stakeholders. For instance, policies, plans and budgets need to align with the available resources and capabilities. Many African governments assume a decentralized approach to education, where the national government establishes standards and policies and the local governments implement these policies and administer schools and education institutions (Republic of Rwanda, 2003). This two-tiered approach to education increases the opportunities for miscommunication and misunderstanding among stakeholders and requires precise coordination in order to reduce inadequacies. In order to effect positive changes, Africa can consider developed countries as a model for collaborative efforts. For instance, Sattler (2011) discusses the implementation of work-integrated learning in Ontario's postsecondary sector. This initiative included collaboration amongst several stakeholders, including students, institutions, employers, and community organizations, to provide students with applied learning opportunities in the classroom, community, and industry (Sattler, 2011). At the same time, however, Teferra and Greijn (2010) suggest that African nations create their own knowledge, information, and technology. These increased innovations would improve both the education system by providing the government with culturally based knowledge on the effective structuring of the education system (Teferra & Greijn, 2010; United Nations University, 2008). Some other improvements suggested in the literature include accountability, target setting, monitoring tools, regulation methods, compliance of individual institutions, and quality assurance (DFID, 2012; Materu, 2007).

Furthermore, authentic learning initiatives can assist in bridging the gap between stakeholders, especially in connecting students and schools to potential employers. One authentic learning tool that can incorporate multiple stakeholders involves the use of the professional portfolio. Clementz and Pitt (2002) describe this tool as a means by which students can exhibit their abilities and achievements to various stakeholders, including instructors, preceptors, supervisors, employers, admissions committees, and graduate schools. The portfolio displays authentic learning through its incorporation of many artifacts that connect student work to the real world: work samples, photographs, digital media, recommendations, field notes, and student transcripts (Clementz & Pitt, 2002). The use of technology can also facilitate stakeholder connections; digital media, such as mobile and computing technologies, can enable students to share their work with teachers, parents, governmental members, community organizations, and even corporations (Traxler & Dearden, 2005). A 2011 report by the United Nations stated that private sector companies have the ability to contribute to education by sharing their knowledge of labor trends, such as emerging sectors, shortages or surpluses, and changing occupational requirements. Among all stakeholders, the government needs to make the first step towards revising postsecondary education to align more closely with the modern labor market and include authentic learning initiatives. At the same time, however, if Ken Robinson's metaphor holds true, small changes at any level of the system are better than stagnation.

CONCLUSION

This book has advocated for the inclusion of authentic learning in the postsecondary education of African nations with the objective of preparing students for the emerging creative economy. As described by award-winning Canadian educator Steve Revington, authentic learning involves a relatively modern approach to education that provides real-world tasks targeting essential skills such as critical thinking, creativity, problem solving, innovation, communication, and collaboration. While educators should implement authentic learning at all levels of schooling, this approach is needed most urgently at the postsecondary level, as these students are the closest to entering the workforce and hence most vital to the economy. In the newly-emerging creative economy, employers require university and college graduates with employable skills that they can transfer immediately from the classroom to the workplace environment or that can allow them to explore the possibility of entrepreneurship. While previous resource-based or manufacturing economies focused on teaching students isolated skills with a regimented environment, the current knowledge-based economy focuses on the development of skills that allow students to manipulate knowledge and transfer their abilities from one job or industry to another.

Authentic learning not only supports and nurtures students to develop these soft skills but also provides numerous benefits to all stakeholders, including students, teachers, educational administrators, employers, the government, and the economy as a whole. Although the SSA region lags behind the rest of the world in terms of its education and economy, its workforce has evolved to begin the first steps towards incorporating a creative economy that necessitates employees with employable skills and focuses heavily on startups and entrepreneurship. Unfortunately, the education systems in African nations, especially the postsecondary or tertiary levels, still require modification to incorporate increased authentic learning opportunities, which partially results from a lack of financial, material, and technological resources. While some efforts have been made to address this need, these initiatives have been fragmented, failing to result in wholesale changes.

Thus, African postsecondary institutions require organized collaboration from all stakeholders to implement authentic learning opportunities.

The first step in such a collaborative effort must begin with the governments of the respective SSA countries initiating dialogue about the creation of a centralized educational policy. In particular, this policy must address all of the previous areas required for establishing authentic learning at African postsecondary institutions: funding, resources, technology, curriculum, and teacher training. Prior to creating such a policy, however, it is important that all stakeholders in our audience, including government, educational administration, employers, teachers, parents, and students, understand the need to implement change and adopt a positive mindset towards the required modifications. As some of my interviewees revealed, many people, especially in the education industry, tend to resist change. Hopefully this book has helped to mitigate such resistance by opening people's eyes about the dire state of education in SSA and the fact that all levels of schooling not only fail to contribute to society but also, in many ways, represent a liability to the extent that school prevents many students from realizing their dreams. As a primary school student in Uganda, I lost two valuable opportunities: one to link my education to Ugandan agriculture, a major industry in SSA yet one that demonstrates significant skill deficits, and another to collaborate with my friend to become an entrepreneur. The emerging creative economy in African nations can certainly benefit from more startups, yet outmoded education systems clearly impede students from carving their niche in life and the African economies from progressing beyond third world countries.

Stakeholders from outside of SSA, especially the governments and educational administrators in western countries, can help by realizing the need to direct funding and resources towards education in SSA. At the same time, the governments of SSA and the respective ministries of education need to develop more efficient planning that utilizes these funds to specifically target the aforementioned deficits. Some of the identified areas that require targeting include infrastructure, especially wireless internet service, as well as technology and resources, such as computers, smartboards, mobile phones, and tablets. Additional funds should be devoted towards improved teacher training methods and increased compensation for teachers, thereby motivating them to not only show up to their classrooms but also spend time and effort in devising effective learning activities. Moreover, the efficient utilization of existing resources, as shown in Chapter 5, can still result in authentic learning with positive outcomes. Furthermore, external stakeholders can ideally consider the shared use of open-source learning materials, which teachers, instructors, and students in SSA can access free of charge. Finally, the curriculum planners need to revise the curricula for each subject and grade level, including postsecondary education, to permit and even require the use of authentic learning. With policies that mandate authentic learning, improved teacher training, altered curricula that permit authentic learning opportunities, and adequate infrastructure and materials, the opportunities are endless.

I am not naïve enough to imagine that such dramatic changes will occur in short order or without any significant obstacles. But my education, direct experience, and extensive research, has taught me that change is possible and that the mere thought of obstacles should not paralyze the stakeholders from attempting this challenging yet game-changing endeavor. This book has provided evidence that it is possible to reform education throughout SSA and that the time, effort, and short-term setbacks will not deter it from happening. As Ken Robinson pointed out, everyone takes some share of the responsibility within the organic, interdependent system of education and society. While none of us can do it alone, we can all play our part in this necessary change. The government, in collaboration with ministries of education, educational administrators, and industry, can establish guidelines that align education with labor force needs and mandate that students learn the real-world skills of collaboration, innovation, creativity, problem solving, and communication. Curriculum developers can set objectives for each grade level and subject matter that teach students not only relevant, real-world topics but also the soft skills that characterize the creative economy. Educational administrators can create teacher education programs that establish a greater link between theory and practice while instructing students on student-centered paradigms such as authentic learning. Employers from various sectors of the economy should prioritize opening doors and creating adequate spaces for students who are yearning for meaningful learning to equip themselves with real-life skills. Finally, teachers can enhance their own education to keep abreast of new research and modify their teaching style to adopt authentic learning while collaborating with industry to guide students towards their professional career or startup venture.

Before any of that can happen, however, the process of initiating dialogue remains the first step to achieving this crucial transformation. Although conversation is only the first step towards change, it represents a necessary starting point in closing the persistent gap between schools and the real world while providing students with the skills to succeed in real life. Let's stop making fish climb trees and start teaching them to swim.

REFERENCES

Academia Group. (2016, March 9). How do we better support students in times of transition? *Academia Forum*. Retrieved from http://forum.academica.ca/forum/smoothing-out-the-continuum-how-do-we-better-support-students-in-times-of-transition

Academica Group. (2017, February 9). Canada must bolster skills training as jobs are lost to automation, says economic council head. *Academica Group*. Retrieved from http://www.academica.ca/top-ten/canada-must-bolster-skills-training-jobs-are-lost-automation-says-economic-council-head?utm_source=Academica+Top+Ten&utm_campaign=5cbc05da03-EMAIL_CAMPAIGN_2017_02_28&utm_medium=email&utm_term=0_b4928536cf-5cbc05da03-47780753

Adeyemi, M.B., & Adeyinka, A.A. (2002). Some key issues in African traditional education. *McGill Journal of Education, 37*(2), 223-240.

AIR. (2013). Are personalized learning environments the next wave of K-12 education reform? *Education Issue Paper Series*. American Institutes for Research.

Algonquin College. (2016, February 11). New centre "ignites" innovation and entrepreneurship at Algonquin College. *Algonquin College*. Retrieved from http://www.algonquincollege.com/public-relations/2016/02/11/new-centre-ignites-innovation-and-entrepreneurship-at-algonquin-college/

Alidou, H., Boly, A., Brock-Utne, B., Diallo, Y.S., Heugh, K., & Ekkehard Wolff, H. (2006). Optimizing Learning and Education in Africa: The Language Factor. *Association for the Development of Education in Africa (ADEA) UNESCO Institute for Education*. ADEA Biennial Meeting. Libreville, Gabon, March 27-31, 2006.

Alstete, J. (2008). Aspects of entrepreneurial success. *Journal of Small Business and Enterprise Development, 15*(3), 584-594.

Anderson, R. (2010). The "idea of a university" today. *History and Policy*. Retrieved from http://www.historyandpolicy.org/policy-papers/papers/the-idea-of-a-university-today

Athabasca University. (2017). Scheduling and timelines. *Athabasca University.* Retrieved from http://www.athabascau.ca/discover/how-au-works/scheduling-and-timelines/

Atkinson, E. (2011). *Learning approaches and technology trends.* St. Johns, Newfoundland: Memorial University.

Banas, J.R., & York, C.S. (2014). Authentic learning exercises as a means to influence preservice teachers' technology integration self-efficacy and intentions to integrate technology. *Australasian Journal of Educational Technology, 30*(6), 728-746.

Barnes, V., Gachago, D., & Ivala, E. (2012). Digital storytelling and authentic learning: A case study in Industrial Design. Proceedings of *Design, Development & Research Conference.* Cape Town, South Africa. September 4-5, 2012.

Barron, B., & Darling-Hammond, L. (2008). *Teaching for meaningful learning: A review of research on inquiry-based and cooperative learning.* Stanford University: The George Lucas Educational Foundation.

Bar-Yam, M., Rhoades, K., Sweeney, L.B., Kaput, J., & Bar-Yam, Y. (2002). Changes in the teaching and learning process in a complex education system. *New England Complex Systems Institute: Solving Problems of Science and Society.* Retrieved from http://www.necsi.edu/research/management/education/teachandlearn.html

Bell, S. (2010). Project-based learning for the 21st century: Skills for the future. *The Clearing House, 83*, 39-43.

Binagwaho, A., Kyamanywa, P., Farmer, P.E., Nuthulaganti, T., Umbubyeyi, R.N., Nyemazi, J.P,....Goosby, E. (2013). The human resources for health program in Rwanda: A new partnership. *The New England Journal of Medicine, 369*(21), 2054-2059

Bloom, D., Canning, D., & Chan, K. (2006). *Higher education and economic development in Africa.* Human Development Sector: Africa Region. Boston, MA: Harvard University.

Bocconi, S., Kampylis, P.G., & Punie, Y. (2012). *Innovating learning: Key elements for developing creative classrooms in Europe.* JRC Scientific and Policy Reports. Spain: European Commission Joint Research Center.

Borrows, J. (2006, December). *Indigenous environmental laws: Purpose, scope, recognition, interpretation, and enforcement.* Victoria, BC: Centre for Indigenous Environmental Resources (CIER).

Bountrogianni, M. (2015, July 8). Six ways continuing education can close Canada's skills gap. *Huff Post.* Retrieved from http://www.huffingtonpost.ca/dr-marie-bountrogianni/adult-education-second-career_b_7737592.html

Bozalek, V., Gachago, D., Alexander, L., Watters, K., Wood, D., Ivala, E...Herrington, J. (2013). The use of emerging technologies for authentic learning: A South African study in higher education. *British Journal of Educational Technology, 44*(4), 629-638.

British Council. (2014). Can higher education solve Africa's job crisis? Understanding graduate employability in Sub-Saharan Africa. *Going Global 2014.* British Council.

Bunoti, S. (2010). The quality of higher education in developing countries needs professional support. *Center for Education Innovations: An Initiative of Results for Development Institute.* 1-10.

Busl, G. (2015, October 19). Humanities research is groundbreaking, life-changing...and ignored. *The Guardian.* Retrieved from http://www.theguardian.com/higher-education-network/2015/oct/19/humanities-research-is-groundbreaking-life-changing-and-ignored

Campbell, A. (2013). Building a multi-language database of video explanations for first year mathematics. Conference Proceedings from *Higher Education Learning and Teaching Association of Southern Africa.* Stellenbosch University, South Africa. November 28-30 2012.

Carleton University. (2016). Bachelor of Computer Science Internship. *School of Computer Science.* Retrieved from https://carleton.ca/scs/future-students/undergraduate/bcs-internship/

Charbonneau, L. (2009). So, you want to be an AUCC member? *University Affairs.* Retrieved from http://www.universityaffairs.ca/opinion/margin-notes/so-you-want-to-be-an-aucc-member/

Choise, S. (2015, October 28). Canadian universities want to increase private sector partnerships. *The Globe and Mail.* Retrieved from http://www.theglobeandmail.com/news/national/canadian-universities-commit-to-helping-students-gain-real-world-experience/article27010871/

Clementz, A.R., & Pitt, R. (2002). *Student portfolios and authentic learning outcomes assessment.* Faculty Development Center: Bryant College.

Conejar, R.J., & Kim, H.K. (2014). The effect of future mobile learning: Current state and future opportunities. *International Journal of Software Engineering and its Applications, 8*(8), 193-200.

Contact North (2015). *The future of higher education: A Canadian view.* Toronto, ON: Contact North.

Cote, J., & Allahar, A. (2008). Response to 'Anxious Academics: Mission Drift and Sliding Standards in the Canadian University.'" *Canadian Journal of Sociology* 33(2): 418-420.

Craig, G. (2007). Community capacity-building: Something old, something new...? *Critical Social Policy, 27*(3), 335-359.

Cram, D. (2014). *Innovation management*. British Columbia: Okanagan University.

CRD. (2013, April 8). 2013 Ready, set, solve program provides real-world solutions. *Capital Region District*. Retrieved from https://www.crd.bc.ca/about/news/2013/04/08/2013-ready-set-solve.

Damoense, M. Y. (2003). Online learning: Implications for effective learning for higher education in South Africa. *Australaisan Journal of Educational Technology, 19*(1).

DFID. (2012). *DFID's Education Programmes in Three East African Countries*. Independent Commission for Aid Impact. Report 10 – May 2012.

Diamond, J., & Gonzalez, P.C. (2014). *Digital badges for teacher mastery: An exploratory study of a competency-based professional development badge system*. CCT Reports. New York, NY: Education Development Center/ Center for Children & Technology.

Dion, J., Cantinotti, M., Ross, A., & Collin-Vezina, D. (2015). Sexual abuse, residential schooling and probably pathological gambling among Indigenous Peoples. *Child Abuse & Neglect, 44*, 56-65.

Dobbin, F. (2009). How Durkheim's theory of meaning-making influenced organizational society. In Paul S. Adler (Ed.), *The Oxford Handbook of Sociology and Organization Studies: Classical Foundations* (pp. 200-222). London: Oxford University Press.

Doyle, M.E., & Smith, M.K. (2007). Jean-Jacques Rousseau on nature, wholeness, and education. *The encyclopedia of informal education*. Retrieved from http://infed.org/mobi/jean-jacques-rousseau-on-nature-wholeness-and-education/

EFA. (2014). *Teaching and Learning: Achieving Quality for All*. EFA Global Monitoring Report.

Engelmann, S., & Carnine, D. (2011). *Could John Stuart Mill have saved our schools?* Verona, WI: Full Court Press

Errington, E.P. (2011). Mission possible: Using near-world scenarios to prepare graduates for the professions. *International Journal of Teaching and Learning in Higher Education, 23*(1), 84-91.

European Commission. (2014). High level group on the modernization of higher education. *Report to the European Commission on New Modes of Learning and Teaching in Higher Education*.

Faulkner, K., & Faulkner, N.J.G. (2012). Designing and supporting collaborative learning activities. Proceedings from *the 44rth ACM Technical Symposium on Computer Science Education*. Denver, CO: SIGCSE (pp. 537-538.)

Fishman, B., & Holman, C. (2015, December 1). Barry Fishman and Caitlin Holman: Higher ed grading systems deserve an F. *It's Not Academic*. Higher Education Quality Council of Ontario. Retrieved from http://blog-en.heqco.ca/2015/12/barry-fishman-and-caitlin-holman-higher-ed-grading-systems-deserve-an-f/

Florida, R., & Spencer, G. (2015, October 7). Canada's urban competitiveness agenda: Completing the transition from a resource to a knowledge economy. *Insight: Canada's urban competitiveness agenda*. Retrieved from http://martinprosperity.org/content/canadas-urban-competitiveness-agenda/

Frey, B.B., Schmitt, V.L., & Allen, J.P. (2012). Defining authentic classroom assessment. *Practical Assessment, Research & Evaluation 17*(2), 1-18.

Fry, H., Ketteridge, S., & Marshall, S (2009). A handbook for teaching and learning in higher education: Enhancing academic practice (3rd ed.). New York and London: Routledge.

Fulford, G. (2007). *Sharing our success: More case studies in Aboriginal schooling*. Kelowna, BC: Society for the Advancement of Excellence in Education.

Galgonovicz, J.P. (2000). *The educational theory of Thomas Aquinas (1225-1274)*. Retrieved from http://www.newfoundations.com/GALLERY/Aquinas.html

Gambhir, M., Broad, K., Evans, M., & Gaskell, J. (2008). The models of teacher education. *Characterizing initial teacher education in Canada: Themes and issues*. Toronto: University of Toronto.

Gardner, H. (2011). *Frames of mind: The theory of multiple intelligences*. Basic Books.

Garry, A., & Phillips, J. (2013). Navigating the future. *Personalize learning*. Dell, Inc.

Global Black History. (2016). History and outcomes of colonial education in Africa. Global Black History. Retrieved from http://www.globalblackhistory.com/2016/07/history-outcomes-colonial-education-africa.html

Goulet, J. H., Charles, C. Z., & Triplett, S. G. (2016). *Creative state: 2016 creative industries report*. Michigan: Creative State Michigan.

Gray, P. (2008, August 20). A brief history of education. *Psychology Today*. Retrieved from https://www.psychologytoday.com/blog/freedom-learn/200808/brief-history-education

Guisepi, R. (2007). The history of education. *History World International*. Retrieved from http://history-world.org/history_of_education.htm

Har, L.B. (2005). Authentic learning. *The Active Classroom*. Retrieved from https://www.eduhk.hk/aclass/Theories/AuthenticLearning_28June.pdf

Harford, E. (2016). The Canadian dream: One millennial's rejection of university's 'industrial repetition.' *Ottawa Citizen*. Retrieved from http://ottawacitizen.com/news/local-news/the-canadian-dream-one-millennials-rejection-of-universitys-industrial-repetition

Havergal, C. (2016, January 9). Universities 'must prepare students for a globalized world.' *Times Higher Education*. Retrieved from https://www.timeshighereducation.com/news/momodou-sallah-universities-must-prepare-students-for-a-globalised-world

Hein, G.E. (1999). Is meaning making constructivism? Is constructivism meaning making? *National Association for Museum Exhibition*.

Helm, J.H. (2008). Got standards: Don't give up on engaged learning. *Beyond the Journal: Young Children on the Web*. National Association for the Education of Young Children.

Herrington, J. (2009). Authentic e-learning in higher education. *eLi 2009 Riyadh Conference*. Murdoch, Australia.

Herrington, A., & Herrington, J. (2006). What is an authentic learning environment? In A. Herrington & J. Herrington (Eds.), *Authentic learning environments in higher education* (pp. 1-14). Australia: IGI Global.

Herrington, A., & Herrington, J. (2007). Authentic mobile learning in higher education. Paper presented at the AARE Annual Conference. Fremantle.

Herrington, J., & Kervin, L. (2007). Authentic learning supported by technology: Ten suggestions and cases of integration in classrooms. *Educational Media International, 44*, 1-20.

Herrington, J., Parker, J., & Boase-Jelinek, D. (2014). Connected authentic learning: Reflection and intentional learning. *Australian Journal of Education, 58*(1), 23-35.

Herrington, J., Reeves, T.C., Oliver, R., & Woo, Y. (2004). Designing authentic activities in web-based courses. *Journal of Computing in Higher Education, 16*(1), 3-29.

Hewitt, A. (2016, March). *Developing Canada's future workforce: A survey of large private-sector employers*. Business Council of Canada. Retrieved from http://thebusinesscouncil.ca/wp-content/uploads/2016/02/Developing-Canadas-Workforce-March.pdf

Higgins, P., & Nicol, R. (2002). *Outdoor education: Authentic learning in the context of landscapes*. (Vol 2). Kisa, Sweden.

Hill, A.M., & Smith, H.A. (1998). Practice meets theory in technology education: A case of authentic learning in the high school setting. *Journal of Technology Education, 9*(2), 29-45.

Hivos. (2016). *The status of the creative economy in East Africa*. Hivos: People Unlimited.

Hogan, P., Carlson, B., & Kirk, C. (2015). Open educational practices' models using open education resources. Proceedings from *Open Educational Global 2015: Innovation and Entrepreneurship*. Banff, AB, Canada.

Howkins, J. (2013). *The creative economy: How people make money from ideas* (2nd ed.). New York, NY: Penguin.

Hui, F., & Koplin, M. (2011). The implementation of authentic activities for learning: A case study in finance education. *E-Journal of Business Education & Scholarship of Teaching, 5*(1), 59-72.

Humes, L.R. (2013). *The need for new paradigms in education*. IMS Global Learning Consortium Series on Learning Impact. Global Learning Consortium.

Hummel, C. (1993). Aristotle. *Prospects,* 23(1/2), 39-51. UNESCO International Bureau of Education.

Israel, S. (2017, March 5). Canada's sharing economy is growing – but should we really call it 'sharing'? *CBC News*. Retrieved from http://www.cbc.ca/news/business/statistics-canada-sharing-economy-1.4004993

IUCEA. (2014). Report from a Study Establishing the Status of Higher Education Qualifications Systems and their Contributions to Human Resources Development in East Africa. *Inter-University Council for East Africa*. Kampala, Uganda.

Jaffer, S., Ng'ambi, D., & Czerniewicz, L. (2007). The role of ICTs in higher education in South Africa: One strategy for addressing teaching and learning challenges. *IJEDICT, 3*(4), 131-142.

Jones, S.M., Casper, R., Dermoudy, J., Osborn, J., & Yates, B. (2010). Authentic learning: A paradigm for increasing student motivation in an era of mass education. *Conference: Teaching Matters*. University of Tasmania. 1-8.

Juma, C. (September 5, 2014). *Reinventing Africa's Universities*. Aljazeera. Retrieved from http://www.aljazeera.com/indepth/opinion/2014/09/reinventing-africa-universities-2014959207677854.html

Jumani, R., & Jumani, Y. (2013). Constructing authentic curriculum context for relevance and sustainability: Transforming roles of educational leaders as authentic pedagogues. *International Researcher, 2*(3), 118-124.

Kampylis, P., & Berki, E. (2014). *Nurturing Creative Thinking*. Geneva, Switzerland, International Academy of Education.

Kandiero, A., & Jagero, N. (2014). Leveraging emerging technologies to address specific learning challenges and derive authentic learning in mathematics for business at Africa University – Zimbabwe. *International Journal of Academic Research in Progressive Education and Development, 3*(1), 172-181,

Kangai, R., & Bukaliya, R. (2011). Teacher development through open and distance learning. *International Journal on New Trends in Education and their Implications, 2*(4), 124-141.

Kanuka, H., & Nocente, N. (2002). Professional development in the online classroom. *CJSAE/RCEEA 16*(1), 34-55.

Kanuka, H. (2008). Understanding e-learning technologies-in-practice through philosophies-in-practice. In T. Anderson (Ed.), *The theory and practice of online learning* (2nd ed., pp. 91-118). Athabasca, Canada: Athabasca University Press.

King. A. (2011). Culture, learning and development: A case study on the Ethiopian higher education system. *Higher Education Research Network Journal, 4*, 5-13.

Knobloch, N. (2003). Is experiential learning authentic? *Journal of Agricultural Education, 44*(4), 22-34.

Kucey, S., & Parsons, J. (2012). Linking past and present: John Dewey and assessment for learning. *Journal of Teaching and Learning, 8*(1), 107-116.

Lawrence, H., Harvey, A., McKnight, J., & Block, P. (2016, March 30). Abundant Community Edmonton. *Abundant Community: Awakening the Power of Families and Neighborhoods*. Retrieved from http://www.abundantcommunity.com/home/posts/friends/parms/1/post/20160330_abundant_community_edmonton.html

Lee, M. (1994). Plato's philosophy of education: Its implication for current education. *Dissertations (1962-2010)*. Retrieved from http://epublications.marquette.edu/dissertations/AAI9517932/

Levasseur, A. (2011, June 13). The case for videogames as powerful tools for learning. *Media Shift*. Retrieved from http://mediashift.org/2011/06/the-case-for-videogames-as-powerful-tools-for-learning164/

Levey, T. G. & Lavin, D. E. (2005). Race and college for all. Paper presented at the Annual Meeting of the American Sociological Association. Philadelphia, PA. 1-21.

Lewis, K. (2008). *Word and world: A critical thinking reader*. Toronto, ON: Nelson Education.

Lewis, L.H., & Williams, C.J. (1994). In L. Jackson & R.S. Caffarella (Eds.), *Experiential Learning: A New Approach* (pp. 5-16). San Francisco, CA: Jossey-Bass.

Locke, J. (1764). *Locke's conduct of the understanding*. Ed. T. Fowler. Oxford: Clarendon Press.

Lombardi, M.M. (2007). Approaches that work: How authentic learning is transforming higher education. *Educase Learning Initiative: Advancing Learning Through IT Innovation*. ELI Paper.

Lulat, Y. G. M. (2005). A history of African higher education from antiquity to the present: A critical synthesis. Westport, CT: Praeger Publishers.

Maina, F.W. (2004). Authentic learning: Perspectives from contemporary educators. *The Journal of Authentic Learning, 1*(1), 1-8.

Majoni, C., & Chinyanganya, T.L. (2014). Integrating traditional African education into current educational practices: Suggestions for primary school pedagogy. *Career Journal of Education and Training Studies, 2*(3), 64-70.

Mamdani, M. (1976). *Politics and class formation in Uganda*. New York: Monthly Review Press.

Mamdani, M. (2000). Key note speech, paper presented at the conference "Social Sciences in the 21st century." Faculty of Social Sciences Makerere University, Kampala, October, 2000.

Mariappan, J., Monemi, S., & Fan, U.J. (2005). Enhancing authentic learning experiences through community-based engineering service learning. *Proceedings of the 2005 American Society of Engineering Education Pacific Southwest Regional ASEE Conference*, Loyola Marymount University, April 7-8.

Materu, P. (2007). Higher education quality assurance in Sub-Saharan Africa: Status, challenges, opportunities, and promising practices. *World Bank Working Paper No. 124*. Washington, DC: The World Bank.

Matsika, C. (2000). *Traditional African education: Its significance to current educational practices with special reference to Zimbabwe*. [Doctoral Dissertation]. Retrieved from http://scholarworks.umass.edu/dissertations/AAI9960770/

Mattar, J.A. (2010). Constructivism and connectivism in education technology: Active, situated, authentic, experiential, and anchored learning. Idaho: Boise State University.

McKenzie, A.D., Morgan, C.K., Cochrane, K.W., Watson, G.K., & Roberts, D.W. Authentic learning: What is it, and what are the ideal curriculum conditions to cultivate it? *HERDSA*. Pp. 426-433.

McLeod, S. (2015). Jean Piaget. *Simply Psychology*. Retrieved from https://www.simplypsychology.org/piaget.html

McTigue, J., Seif, E., & Wiggins, G. (2004). You can teach for meaning. *Teaching for Meaning, 62*(1), 26-31.

Meng, L.J. (2014). Applied Learning Programme (ALP): A possible enactment of achieving authentic learning in Singapore schools. Proceedings from *IAEA 2014: 40th Annual Conference*. Singapore.

Mims, C. (2003). Authentic learning: A practical introduction & guide for implementation. Meridian: A Middle School Computer Technologies Journal, 6(1), 1-12.

Mintz, S. (2016, February 7). Improving rates of success in STEM fields. *Inside Higher Ed*. Retrieved from https://www.insidehighered.com/blogs/higher-ed-beta/improving-rates-success-stem-fields

Miron, D., O'Sullivan, M., & McLoughlin, C. (2000). Authentic student learning: Assisting students to become constructive learners in a first year computer science unit. *The Fourth Pacific Rim – First Year in Higher Education Conference: Creating Futures for a New Millennium*. Queensland University of Technology: Brisbane, Australia.

Moon, J.A. (2004). *A handbook of reflective and experiential learning: Theory and practice*. New York, NY: Routledge.

Moos, D. C., & Honkomp, B. (2014). Adventure learning: Motivating students in a Minnesota Middle School. *Journal of Research on Technology in Education, 43*(3), 231-252.

Mosweunyane, D. (2013). The African educational evolution: From traditional training to formal education. Higher Education Studies, 3(4), 50-59.

Motlhaka, H. A. (2014). Authentic learning: Bridging the gap of knowledge and action in South African higher education. *Mediterranean Journal of Social Sciences, 5*(23), 891-896.

Mugimu, C. B., Nakabugo, M. G., & Katunguka-Rwakishaya, E. (2013). Developing capacity for research and teaching in higher education: A case of Makerere University. *World Journal of Education, 3*(6), 33-45.

Murphy, E. (2007). The end of learning: Milton and education (review). *Renaissance Quarterly, 60*(3), 1048-1049.

Muwagga, M. A. (2006). The Philosophical implications of Liberalization of University Education in *Uganda*. Unpublished doctoral thesis Makerere University Kampala Uganda

Mwinzi, J. M. (2015). Theoretical frameworks and indigenous knowledge systems. International *Journal of Education and Research, 3*(2), 677-684.

Nakkazi, E. (September 19, 2014). *Universities must focus on science, not 'useless' arts*. University World News. Last Viewed February 24, 2015. http://www.universityworldnews.com/article.php?story=20140918151012537

NCHE. (2014). *Ugandan Council for Higher Education*. Kampala, Uganda. Retrieved from http://www.unche.or.ug/institutions

Ndofirepi, A.P., & Ndofirepi, E.S. (2012). (E)ducation or (e)ducation in traditional African societies? A philosophical insight. *Stud Tribes Tribals, 10*(1), 13-28.

Neil, J. (2005). John Dewey, The modern father of experiential education. *Wilderdom*. Retrieved from http://wilderdom.com/experiential/ExperientialDewey.html

Neo, M., Neo, K.T.K., & Tan, H.Y.J. (2012). Applying authentic learning strategies in a multimedia and web learning environment (MWLE): Malaysian students' perspective. *TOJET: The Turkish Online Journal of Education Technology, 11*(3), 50-60.

New African. (2017, May 19). Higher education in Africa: Start of a new golden age? *New African Magazine*. Retrieved from http://newafricanmagazine.com/higher-education-africa-start-new-golden-age/

Newmann, F.M., King, M. B., & Carmichael, D.L. (2007). *Authentic instruction and assessment: Common standards for rigor and relevance in teaching academic subjects.* Des Moines, IA: Iowa Department of Education.

Nikitina, L. (2011). Creating an authentic learning environment in the foreign language classroom. International Journal of Instruction, 4(1), 33-46.

Noddings, N (1995). *Philosophy of education.* Boulder, CO: Westview Press.

Oblinger, D. (2007). Why today's students value authentic learning. *Educase Learning Initiative: Advancing Learning Through IT Innovation.* ELI Paper 9.

Otaala, J., Maani, J.S., & Bakaira, G.G. (2013). Effectiveness of university teacher education curriculum on the secondary school teacher performance in Uganda: The case of Kyambogo University. *Journal of International Cooperation in Education, 15*(3), 95-112.

OPSBA. (2013). *A vision for learning and teaching in the digital age.* Toronto: Ontario Public School Boards' Association.

O'Reilly, T. (2015, July 21). The sharing economy. *CBC Radio.* Retrieved from http://www.cbc.ca/radio/undertheinfluence/the-sharing-economy-1.2983680

Orey, M. (2010). *Global Text: Emerging Perspectives on Learning, Teaching, and Technology.* Zurich, Switzerland, Jacobs Foundation.

Padesky, C. (1993). Socratic questioning: Changing minds or guiding discovery? Keynote address delivered to the European Congress of Behavioural and Cognitive Therapies. London, UK. September 24, 1993. Retrieved from https://padesky.com/newpad/wp-content/uploads/2012/11/socquest.pdf

Paludan, J.P. (2006). Personalized learning 2025. *Personalizing Education.* OECD/CERI.

Parker, J., Maor, D., & Herrington, J. (2013). Authentic online learning: Aligning learner needs, pedagogy and technology. Issues in Educational Research 23(2), 227-241.

Patrick, S. Kennedy, K., & Powell, A. (2013). Mean what you say: Defining and integrating personalized, blended, and competency-based education. New York: iNACOL.

Peritz, I. (2017, September 8). Sir Ken Robinson on how schools are stifling students' creativity. *The Globe and Mail.* Retrieved from https://www.theglobeandmail.com/news/national/education/sir-ken-robinson-on-how-schools-are-stifling-students-creativity/article36205832/

Peterson, M. (2002). *Principles of authentic multi-level instruction.* Detroit, Michigan: Whole Schooling Consortium.

Philby, C. (2013, May 23). Suli Breaks: The secret of success? Forget exams – it's all about getting the breaks. *Independent.* Retrieved from http://www.independent.co.uk/news/people/profiles/suli-breaks-the-secret-of-success-forget-exams-its-all-about-getting-the-breaks-8630036.html

Potts, A., & Schlichting, K.A. (2011). Developing professional forums that support thoughtful discussion, reflection, and social action: One faculty's commitment to social justice and culturally responsive practice. *International Journal of Teaching and Learning in Higher Education, 23*(1), 11-19.

Prince EA. (2016). I just sued the school system. [Web log comment]. Retrieved from https://www.youtube.com/watch?v=dqTTojTija8

Radu, L. (2011). John Dewey and progressivism in American education. *Bulletin of the Transilvania University of Brasov: Series IIV Vol. 4., 53*(2), 85-90.

Reed, D. (2015, November 1). Universities are failing to prepare students for social economy. *Times Higher Education*. Retrieved from https://www.timeshighereducation.com/blog/universities-are-failing-prepare-students-social-economy

Reitsma, G.M., & van Hamburg, E. (2013). Panel members' experience of peer evaluation of teaching practice. Conference Proceedings from *Higher Education Learning and Teaching Association of Southern Africa*. Stellenbosch University, South Africa. November 28-30 2012.

Renzulli, J.S., Gentry, M., & Reis, S.M. (2004). Enrichment clusters news: A time and place for authentic learning. *Educational Leadership.* Association for Supervision and Curriculum Development. 73-77.

Republic of Rwanda. (2003). *Education Sector Policy*. Kigali, Rwanda: Ministry of Education, Science, Technology, and Scientific Research.

Republic of Rwanda Ministry of Health. (2013). *Annual Report: July 2012-June 2013*. Kigali: Ministry of Health.

Resnick, L.B. (1987). Learning in school and out. *Educational Researcher, 16*(9), 13-20.

Revington, S. (2016). *Authentic learning*. Retrieved from http://authenticlearning.weebly.com/

Ricardo, A. (2015, June 26). Why internships are important for students and employers. LinkedIn. Retrieved from https://www.linkedin.com/pulse/why-internships-important-students-employers-andy-ricardo

Rivzi, S.H. (2006). Avicenna/Ibn Sina (CA. 980-1037). *Internet Encyclopedia of Philosophy*. Retrieved from http://www.iep.utm.edu/avicenna/

Robinson, K. (2010, May 24). Bring on the learning revolution. YouTube. Retrieved from https://www.youtube.com/watch?v=r9LelXa3U_I&feature=youtu.be

Robinson, K. (2013, July 18). How to change education. YouTube. Retrieved from https://www.youtube.com/watch?v=BEsZOnyQzxQ&feature=youtu.be

Robinson, N. (2015, September 29). A university degree isn't the only, or best, way to build your earning power. *The Globe and Mail*. Retrieved from http://www.theglobeandmail.com/report-on-business/rob-commentary/a-university-degree-isnt-the-only-or-best-way-to-build-your-earning-power/article26571488/

Rowe, M., Bozalek, V., & Frantz, J. (2013). Using Google Drive to facilitate a blended approach to authentic learning. *British Journal of Educational Technology*, *44*(4), 594-606.

Royal Roads University. (2014). Authentic assessment: What is authentic assessment? *T4T: Tools for Teaching*, *1*(4), 1-4.

Rudman, A. (2013). From passive to active: Active learning methods in international human rights law. Conference Proceedings from *Higher Education Learning and Teaching Association of Southern Africa*. Stellenbosch University, South Africa. November 28-30 2012.

Ruff, C. (2016, January, 13). With new promise by Udacity, money-back guarantee comes to online courses. *The Chronicle of Higher Education*. Retrieved from http://chronicle.com/article/With-New-Promise-by-Udacity/234911

Rule, A. (2006). Editorial: The components of authentic learning. *Journal of Authentic Learning*, *3*(1), 1-10.

Ruto, S., & Rajani, R. (2014). *Are our children learning: Literacy and numeracy across East Africa*. Nairobi, Kenya: Uwezo.

Rwanda Development Board. (2012). *Rwanda skills survey 2012: Construction sector report*. Rwanda: Rwanda Development Board.

Safuan, H.A.J., & Soh, R. (2013). The integration of authentic learning principles and Facebook in service learning. *The Turkish Online Journal of Educational Technology*, *12*(4), 192-199.

Sattler, P. (2011). *Work-Integrated Learning in Ontario's Postsecondary Sector*. Toronto: Higher Education Quality Council of Ontario.

Sawyer, R.K. (2008). *Optimising learning: Implications of learning sciences research*. CERI: Centre for Educational Research and Innovation.

Schlesinger, P. (2016). The creative economy: Invention of a global orthodoxy. Innovation: The *European Journal of Social Science Research*. doi: 10.1080/13511610.2016.1201651

Seidman, R. H. (2016, January 19). Robert H. Seidman – Degree-in-three programs built on competency and assessment. *It's not academic*. Higher Education Quality Council of Ontario. Retrieved from http://blog-en.heqco.ca/2016/01/robert-h-seidman-degree-in-three-programs-built-on-competency-and-assessment/

Shepard, A. (2015, October 30). Opinion: Invest in the next generation, to build a 21st-century knowledge economy. *Montreal Gazette*. Retrieved from http://montrealgazette.com/news/local-news/opinion-invest-in-the-next-generation-to-build-a-21st-century-knowledge-economy

Sherlock, T. (2016). Co-op placements give university students a head start. *Vancouver Sun*. Retrieved from http://www.vancouversun.com/news/metro/placements+give+university+students+head+start/11693032/story.html

Shopify. (2016). Shopify and Carleton are reimagining experiential learning. *Education*. Retrieved from https://www.shopify.ca/education/bcs

Simpson, R. (2013). *Can interactive radio instruction turn post-conflict educational challenges into opportunities*. Retrieved from https://africaeducationaltrust.org/wp-content/uploads/2014/07/2013-Interactive-Radio-Instruction-in-South-Sudan.pdf

Slepkov, H. (2008). *Teacher professional growth in an authentic learning environment*. St. Catharines ON: Brock University.

Smith, A. A. (2015). Working learners. *Inside Higher Ed*. Retrieved from https://www.insidehighered.com/news/2015/10/28/study-calls-stronger-connection-between-jobs-and-education

Ssekamwa, J. C., & Lugumba, S. M. E. (2002). *A history of education in East Africa*. Uganda: Fountain Publishers.

Ssentamu, J.D. (2013). *Prospects and challenges of higher education in Uganda*. Kampala: Makerere University.

Stein, S.J., Isaacs, G., & Andrews, T. (2004). Incorporating authentic learning experiences within a university course. *Studies in Higher Education, 29*(2), 239-258.

Stickel, M., & Liu, (2015). *The Effects of the Inverted Classroom Approach: Student Behaviors, Perceptions and Learning Outcomes*. Toronto, ON: Higher Education Quality Council of Ontario.

Stull, J.C., Varnum, S.J., Ducette, J., Schiller, J., & Bernacki, M. (2011). The many faces of formative assessment. *International Journal of Teaching and Learning in Higher Education, 23*(1), 30-39.

Swaffield, S., Jull, S., & Ampah-Mensah, A. (2013). Using mobile phone texting to support the capacity of school leaders in Ghana to practice leadership for learning. *Procedia – Social and Behavioral Science, 103*, 1295-1302.

Szczepanski, A. (2006). The distinctive nature and potential of outdoor education from a teacher perspective. *Outdoor Education: Authentic Learning in the Context of Landscape Literacy Education and Sensory Experience: Perspective of Where, What, Why, How, and When of Learning Environments*. Interdisciplinary Context and the Outdoor and Indoor Dilemma. 1-18.

Tan, S.K.S., Wong, A.F.L., Gopinathan, S., Goh, K.C., & Wong, I.Y.F (2007). The qualifications of the teaching force: Data from Singapore. In R. M. Ingersoll (Ed.), *A comparative Study of Teacher Preparation and Qualifications in Six Nations* (pp. 71-82) USA: Consortium for Policy Research in Education.

Tedla, E. (1996). *Sankofa: African thought and education*.

Teferra, D., & Greijn, H. (2010). *Higher education and globalization: Challenges, threats, and opportunities for Africa*. Maastricht, Netherlands: Maastricht University.

The Levin Institute. (2015). What is globalization? *Globalization 101*. Retrieved from http://www.globalization101.org/what-is-globalization/

Ti, L.K., Tan, G.M., Khoo, S.G., & Chen, F.G. (2006). The impact of experiential learning on NUS medical students: Our experience with task trainers and human-patient simulation. *ANNALS Academy of Medicine Singapore, 35*, 619-623.

Titus, S. (2013). Mediating authentic learning: The use of wikis and blogs in an undergraduate curriculum in South Africa. *International Conference on Educational Technologies*. Cape Town: South Africa.

Today Media. (2014). UFV and Chinook Helicopters Inc. are joining forces. *Abbottsford Today*. Retrieved from http://www.abbotsfordtoday.ca/ufv-and-chinook-helicopters-ltd-are-joining-forces/?platform=hootsuite

Thinkful. (2016). Learn with the best: 1-on-1 mentorship with industry experts. *Thinkful*. Retrieved from https://www.thinkful.com/

Traxler, J., & Dearden, P. (2005). The potential for using SMS to support learning and organization in Sub-Saharan Africa. *Proceedings of Development Studies Association Conferences, Milton Keynes*.

Turpin, D. (2015, November 16). Opinion: Universities' role in building a better Canada. *Edmonton Journal*. Retrieved from http://edmontonjournal.com/opinion/columnists/opinion-universities-role-in-building-a-better-canada

Tyler, W. (1982). The organizational background of credentialism. *British Journal of Sociology of Education, 3*(2), 161-172.

UNESCO. (2012). Sub-Saharan Africa: 2012 EFA Report. *Global Education for All Meeting*. UNESCO Paris. November 20-13, 2012.

United Nations. (2011). Education challenges in Africa and LDCs. Economic and Social Council High Level Segment: Special Policy Dialogue. United Nations Department of Economic and Social Affairs.

United Nations (2013). *Creative Economy Report 2013 Special Edition: Widening Local Development Pathways*. New York, NY: United Nations Development Programme.

United Nations. (2015). *Creative Economy Outlook and Country Profiles: Trends in international trade and creative industries*. UNCTAD.

United Nations University. (2008). *Revitalizing Higher Education in Sub-Saharan Africa: A United Nations University Project Report*. United Nations.

University Hub. (2016, February 9). Top 10 universities in Canada for future entrepreneurs. *Huffington Post*. Retrieved from http://www.huffingtonpost.ca/universityhubca/universities-for-future-entrepreneurs_b_9190842.

html?utm_content=bufferf8f9b&utm_medium=social&utm_source=twitter.com&utm_campaign=buffer

University of London. (2010). *The role of teachers in improving learning in Burundi, Malawi, Senegal, and Uganda: Great expectations little support*. London, UK: Institute of Education and ActionAid.

UWEZO Publications, (2013, December 16). *Are our children learning? Tanzania Report*. Retrieved from http://www.twaweza.org/go/uwezo-ea-2013-report

Vaisey, S. (2004). Overeducation and its consequences, 1972-2002. Paper presented at the Annual Meeting of the American Sociological Association. San Francisco, CA. 1-20.

Van de Werfhorst, H. G. (2009). Credential inflation and educational strategies: A comparison of the United States and the Netherlands. *Research in Social Stratification and Mobility, 27*, 269-284.

Van de Werfhorst, H. G., & Anderson, R. (2005). Credential inflation and educational strategies. *Acta Sociologica, 48*(4), 321-340.

Vavrus, F., Thomas, M., & Bartlett, L. (2011). *Ensuring quality by attending to inquiry: Learner centered pedagogy in sub-Saharan Africa*. Addis Ababa, UNESCO.

Watkins, K. (2013). Narrowing Africa's education deficit. *Foresight Africa: Top Priorities for the Continent in 2013*. The Brookings Institution: Africa Growth Initiative.

Weingarten, H. P. (2017, February 28). FutureSkillsLab: A step in the right direction. *It's Not Academic*. Retrieved from http://blog-en.heqco.ca/2017/02/harvey-p-weingarten-futureskills-lab-a-step-in-the-right-direction/?utm_source=Academica+Top+Ten&utm_campaign=5cbc05da03-EMAIL_CAMPAIGN_2017_02_28&utm_medium=email&utm_term=0_b4928536cf-5cbc05da03-47780753

Wells, N. (2015, July 24). Indigenous people: Economic conditions. *Historica Canada*. Retrieved from http://www.thecanadianencyclopedia.ca/en/article/aboriginal-people-economic-conditions/

Wesley, C. (2016, July 13). Do you assign enough reading? Or too much? *The Chronicle of Higher Education*. Retrieved from http://chronicle.com/article/Do-You-Assign-Enough-Reading-/237085

West, E.G. (1965). Liberty and education: John Stuart Mill's dilemma. *Liberty, The Journal of the Royal Institute of Philosophy*. Retrieved from https://egwestcentre.files.wordpress.com/2012/07/liberty-and-education.pdf

Westbrook, J., Durrani, N., Brown, R., Orr, D., Pryor, J., Boddy, J., & Salvi, F. (2013). *Pedagogy, Curriculum, Teaching Practices, and Teacher Education in Developing Countries*. United Kingdom: University of Sussex.

Westbrook, R. (1993). John Dewey (1859-1952). *Prospects: The Quarterly Review of Comparative Education, 23*(1/2), 277-291.

Wheeler, D. (2016, January 13). Technology and the imminent disruption of higher education: Is fear the path to the dark side? *Academia Forum.* Retrieved from http://forum.academica.ca/forum/technology-and-the-imminent-disruption-of-higher-education-is-fear-the-path-to-the-dark-side

Wilson, B. G. (1996). *Constructivist learning environments: Case studies in instructional design.* Englewood Cliffs, NJ: Educational Technology Publications.

World Bank. (2011). *Rwanda Education Country Status Report: Toward Quality Enhancement and Achievement of Universal Nine Year Basic Education.* Washington, DC: The International Bank for Reconstruction and Development.

World Economic Forum. (2016). Factors for enabling the creative economy. Geneva Switzerland: World Economic Forum.

Yamada, S. (2007). A history of African higher education from antiquity to the present: A critical synthesis by Y. G. M. Lulat. *The Developing Economics, 45*(2), 245-248.

Younglai, R. (2016, July 13). Low-wage earners with graduate degrees on rise, new study shows. *The Globe and Mail.* Retrieved from http://www.theglobeandmail.com/globe-investor/personal-finance/genymoney/low-wage-earners-with-graduate-degrees-on-rise-new-study-shows/article30892835/

YTC. (2017). About us. Yellowhead Tribal College. Retrieved from https://ytced.ab.ca/about/

Zualkernan, I.A. (2006). A framework and a methodology for developing authentic constructivist e-learning environments. *Educational Technology & Society, 9*(2), 198-212.

Zwiers, J. (2007). Professional development for active learning in Sub-Saharan Africa: Reflectively practicing a community-centered approach. *Journal of Education for International Development, 3*(1), 1-15.

ACKNOWLEDGEMENTS

It is with my deepest gratitude that I thank the many fine people who helped bring *You Can't Make "Fish Climb Trees"* to life.

That would undoubtedly include Professor Heather Kanuka, PhD. A wonderful professor at the University of Alberta, Heather opened my mind, and my heart, to researching teaching and learning, and was a constant pillar of support and encouragement throughout my writing process.

Many thanks also go to the man who pioneered the concept of authentic learning, the inimitable Steve Revington. The impact that Steve has had on my life, and on this book, cannot be measured in mere words, and my gratitude for his help and guidance is profound.

Special thanks also go out to Professors José da Costa, PhD and Darryl Hunter, PhD of the Faculty Education, University of Alberta. Generous and helpful to a fault, their expect advice and guidance were one of my biggest influences, and their staunch support helped me in more ways than I could possibly hope to describe.

Last but certainly not least on my list is Professor Anthony Muwagga Mugagga. Anthony was the missing link, if you will, that allowed me to gain access to the abundance of knowledge, experience and advice of the entire faculty of the College of Education and External Studies at Makerere University. Indeed, *You Can't Make "Fish Climb Trees"* would not exist without the countless hours of deep, introspective conversations I enjoyed with every one of them, conversations that brought true relevance to the book.

It is with the utmost gratitude, respect and humility that I thank all of you, and many others who contributed, from the bottom of my heart.